THE HOLY
COVENANTS

Other Books by the Author

FOR ADULTS

*The Holy Invitation: Understanding
Your Sacred Temple Endowment*

*Repicturing the Restoration:
New Art to Expand Our Understanding*

*Seekers Wanted: The Skills You Need
for the Faith You Want*

Christ in Every Hour

FOR YOUTH

*Q&A: Common Questions and Powerful Answers
for LDS Youth* (with John Hilton III)

*I'm Not Perfect, Can I Still Go to Heaven? Finding Hope for
the Celestial Kingdom through the Atonement of Christ*

THE HOLY COVENANTS

LIVING OUR SACRED TEMPLE PROMISES

ANTHONY SWEAT

DESERET BOOK

SALT LAKE CITY

© 2022 Anthony Sweat

All rights reserved. No part of this book may be reproduced in any form or by any means without permission in writing from the publisher, Deseret Book Company, at permissions@deseretbook.com. This work is not an official publication of The Church of Jesus Christ of Latter-day Saints. The views expressed herein are the responsibility of the author and do not necessarily represent the position of the Church or of Deseret Book Company.

DESERET BOOK is a registered trademark of Deseret Book Company.

Visit us at deseretbook.com

Library of Congress Cataloging-in-Publication Data

Names: Sweat, Anthony, author.

Title: The holy covenants : living our sacred temple promises / Anthony Sweat.

Description: Salt Lake City, Utah : Deseret Book, [2022] | Includes bibliographical references. | Summary: "Popular Latter-day Saint author Anthony Sweat follows up his book The Holy Invitation with The Holy Covenants, teaching how to realize the blessings contained in the covenants made in the temple"—Provided by publisher.

Identifiers: LCCN 2021038244 | ISBN 9781629729794 (trade paperback)

Subjects: LCSH: The Church of Jesus Christ of Latter-day Saints—Doctrines. | Temple endowments (Mormon Church) | Covenants—Religious aspects—The Church of Jesus Christ of Latter-day Saints. | Mormon Church—Doctrines.

Classification: LCC BX8643.T4 S939 2022 | DDC 246/.9589332—dc23

LC record available at https://lccn.loc.gov/2021038244

Printed in the United States of America
Brigham Young University Press, Provo, UT

To Cindy,
my eternal covenant companion
in the holy order.

CONTENTS

Author's Note — ix

PART I: THE ORDER
The Order of the Son of God — 3
The White Coat Parable — 15
The Why of Covenants — 27

PART II: THE COVENANTS
The Commitment to Wear the Garment — 43
The Promise to Not Reveal Sacred Teachings — 52
The Law of Obedience — 59
The Law of Sacrifice — 67
The Law of the Gospel — 74

CONTENTS

The Law of Chastity	81
The Law of Consecration	91

PART III: THE POWER

The Endowment of Power	105
The Taste of Eternity	113
Notes	125

AUTHOR'S NOTE

If you're reading this book, it's likely you want to better grasp what the endowment and its covenants are about. Regardless of your age or temple experience, understanding and living temple promises is crucial to becoming endowed with heavenly power in everyday life. This book is meant as a companion to my earlier book, *The Holy Invitation*. If you haven't read it, I might suggest you do. It isn't necessary to have read *The Holy Invitation* to understand and get a lot out of what you're about to read here, but it will give you some big-picture perspectives to understand the temple endowment.

One book can't address every need, and while I believe *The Holy Invitation* does its job well, it falls short

AUTHOR'S NOTE

in that it doesn't go into the covenants of the temple, what those covenants may mean, why they matter, or how to consider living them. In other words, *The Holy Invitation* helps you understand the endowment, but not necessarily how to become *endowed*. There is a difference, you know, in receiving your temple endowment—or participating in the ceremony—and becoming "endowed with power from on high" (D&C 38:32) in your life. We have to pursue receiving the endowment of power in a similar way we pursue receiving the Holy Ghost. Just because we've participated in the ordinance doesn't necessarily give us the power. Where *The Holy Invitation* is meant to help you better prepare to understand the endowment, *The Holy Covenants* is meant to help you better become endowed with power.

With that goal in mind, I've written and divided this book into three parts: The Order, The Covenants, and The Power. Part I, The Order, seeks to give you a theological framework to the temple's teachings, including a parable to help connect some overall ideas together. Similar to my approach with the parable in *The Holy Invitation*, I do not interpret this fictional story for you (I feel it is more impactful if you do that yourself), although there are subtle hints in the form of reused phrases throughout the book. Part II, The

AUTHOR'S NOTE

Covenants, examines five major temple covenants we make—the laws of obedience, sacrifice, the gospel, chastity, and consecration—along with two associated commitments: to wear the temple garment and not reveal sacred temple teachings. These chapters are deep and doctrinal but are also a bit more practical. I divide each covenant chapter into an "Explanation" (what), an "Application" (how), and a "Motivation" (why) to help portion information into more digestible pieces. Part III, The Power, concludes the book with how living these covenants can bless and empower us on earth and in heaven, along with a more personal closing essay illustrating how the endowment can help us glimpse our true eternal identity.

In this book I seek to be appropriately open, teaching earnestly and accessibly about the temple,[1] but also sensitively and sacredly. There's no perfect balance there, and admittedly I may tip too far one way or another, saying too little in one place or more than you may prefer somewhere else. Please be assured that the major ideas I cover herein have been publicly discussed by Church leadership or published by the institutional Church. In this book I cite where all those major doctrines, phrases, or covenants are found. Sometimes I quote directly if the words are needed or are beautiful—more powerfully or better said than

AUTHOR'S NOTE

I could. However, to avoid this book becoming too "quote heavy," I do not quote every concept. I want this to be readable, and sometimes paragraphs that are constantly bracketed by quotes become tiresome. This book seeks to synthesize the citations into readable sentences.

Thus, these are my words and interpretations gleaned from those public sources. While I strive for truth, I do not presume to have a complete understanding of these concepts, and acknowledge I may be unintentionally amiss or uninformed in certain areas. This book reflects many years of my personal learning, teaching, and worship, but I yet look forward to growing in my own understanding of the temple and its covenants by degrees, as the temple ceremony itself suggests. I seek to be faithful and loyal to the Church and its leaders that I love, but I do not presume to speak for the Church, Brigham Young University, Deseret Book, nor anyone other than myself. My greatest desire is that the ideas in this book may, in some measure, help you or a loved one better grasp the grand beauties of the temple and become endowed more fully by its spiritual power.

PART I

THE ORDER

"Now Melchizedek was a man of faith, who wrought righteousness; . . . and thus, having been approved of God, he was ordained a high Priest, after the order of the covenant which God made with Enoch; it being after the order of the Son of God."

—JOSEPH SMITH

THE ORDER OF THE SON OF GOD

Let's start by trying to get something in order.

If you heard a group of people say, "We're ordering this," what would they mean?

Without any context, it's difficult to say, isn't it? It could mean they want to purchase something, like placing an order online. Maybe they are at a restaurant and are requesting a food order. "I want to order this" could mean they want to organize something, like the tools in their garage. Perhaps they need to put something in a sequence of steps, like the "order of operations" in math, where you start with parentheses. Maybe they are leaders issuing a command for required action: "That's an order!" There are lots of different ways to order the word *order*.

THE HOLY COVENANTS

When Joseph Smith and the early Saints first built a temple, Jesus revealed that it was to be a "house of order" (D&C 88:119). We usually interpret that as something like a house of organization or a house of neatness. Those are proper applications, but they may not be the only ways to read it. "Order" can also imply something more, like a house of sequence. We see this type of progressive "house of order" in military ranks or school degrees from a bachelor's to a master's to a doctorate. A temple being a "house of order" could mean a house of progression, like how one progresses through the order of the priesthood (Aaronic to Melchizedek) or in glory from telestial to terrestrial to celestial.

Related to this, *order* can also mean a select or classified group. That definition should be familiar to you who have read books like *Harry Potter and the Order of the Phoenix*. That's fictional, but in real life there are actual orders of knights, animal hunters, martial artists, and more. These orders usually consist of people who have been inducted into a society or group that has some sort of unique identity or mission. This latter definition is one we should carefully consider when we think about the temple. The Lord's house is not only a house creating order; it's also a house creating *an* order. A new, ancient order.

THE ORDER OF THE SON OF GOD

A NEW, ANCIENT ORDER

When Joseph Smith endowed the first people in Nauvoo in the 1840s, they became known as "the anointed quorum" or the "holy order."[1] This holy order was full of faithful women, such as Emma Smith, Vilate Kimball, and Phoebe Woodruff, and men, including Orson Pratt, William Clayton, and W. W. Phelps, each of whom had been washed, anointed, instructed, and sealed in sacred ceremonies[2] to become high priestesses and priests. They were part of a select group who had received "the communication of Keys pertaining to the Aaronic Priesthood, and so on to the highest order of Melchisedec Priesthood . . . setting forth the order pertaining to the Ancient of Days," as Joseph Smith explained, so that they could gain spiritual power and capacity, come into the presence of God, and receive a fulness of His exalted blessings.[3]

Ever since June of 1831, the Prophet Joseph had been working toward this goal, seeking to help Church members become great modern high priests like Melchizedek, able to access the powers of heaven. The word *endowment* is commonly defined today in the Church as a "gift,"[4] but importantly, the word *endowment* also means a capacity, power, or ability.[5] At this June 1831 conference, the Lord through His prophet desired to give some faithful Saints divine capacity, power, and ability—or, an "endowment."[6] There, Joseph ordained the first men in this dispensation to be high priests after the order of Melchizedek.[7] He promised them power from this high priestly order—power to perform miracles;[8] power to seal people up to eternal life;[9] power like ancient apostles[10] and prophets; power to "break mountains" and "divide the seas" and "put at defiance the armies of nations" (JST, Genesis 14:30–31).

John Corrill, who was present at the June 1831 conference, connected this high priesthood power with the order of Melchizedek, recalling, "The [Melchizedek] priesthood was then for the first time introduced, and conferred on several of the elders. In this chiefly consisted the endowment—it being a new order—and bestowed authority."[11] This new order of Melchizedek's priesthood was for a person to become "an high priest after the order of the covenant which God made with Enoch" (JST, Genesis 14:27), or "after the Order of the Son of God" (D&C 107:3).

Joseph didn't desire to make only a few of his inner circle part of this holy order; he wanted all Saints to be similarly endowed as soon as they were prepared.[12] He told the women of the Nauvoo Relief Society that he "was going to make of this Society a kingdom of

Priests as in Enoch's day."[13] Years earlier, the Prophet had organized the School of the Prophets to prepare men to become endowed, and now Phoebe Woodruff likened the Relief Society to a female school of the prophets[14] to prepare the sisters for the temple endowment, just as had been done for the elders. God wanted to make every Saint part of this holy order, a "kingdom of priests" (Exodus 19:6), women and men together—covenant Saints who are set apart from the base things of the world and dedicated to serving the Lord, building His kingdom, creating Zion, and fulfilling His plan; who understand how to discern between right and wrong, recognize God's voice, receive divine answers, hearken to His servants, commune with angels, and come into the presence of God; who know how to tap into the powers of heaven and live a celestial, exalted life. And that's where you and I come in. We, too, can be part of this holy order.

THE ORDER OF THE SON OF GOD

The scriptures often speak about the "holy order of the Son of God" or the "order of Melchizedek."[15] Let's not be too intimidated or overwhelmed by these phrases. Think of the word *order* using its synonyms I previously mentioned, like *pattern*, *system*, or *a select group of people*.[16] It's a pattern of righteous living—entered into by priesthood covenants—to create a holy group of Saints who live after the manner of Jesus, the Son of God. Today, we are initiated into this sacred order of priests and priestesses through the ordinances and covenants of the holy temple.

To be clear, in some contexts this priesthood order is discussed as men being ordained to certain priesthood *offices* in the Church through the laying on of hands (see Alma 13:1; D&C 107:10). While that is accurate, remember there are many ways to order the word *order*. Entering the holy order of the Son of God is also undertaken through making and keeping priesthood covenants and ordinances, including the washing and anointing, endowment ceremony, and eternal marriage sealing, which in scripture is called an "order of the priesthood" (D&C 131:2). President Ezra Taft Benson summarized, "To enter into the order of the Son of God is the equivalent today of entering into the fulness of the Melchizedek Priesthood, which is only received in the house of the Lord."[17] In fact, seeing the holy order through the lens of the temple broadens our vision of priesthood to apply to all members, including women. When we view entering into the holy order of the Son of God through receiving temple ordinances and keeping temple covenants, it becomes a way for all to enjoy the gifts, power, authority, and blessings of

THE ORDER OF THE SON OF GOD

the holy priesthood, as modern prophets have pled for us to better understand.[18] We can see how priesthood isn't only an ecclesiastical office for men; it's a covenant order for us all.

Thus, Adam and Eve[19] entered into and lived after this order; so did Abraham and Sarah and Joseph and Emma.[20] Moses sought to have his people enter into God's "holy order . . . and the ordinances thereof," but through disobedience they lost their opportunity (JST, Exodus 34:1–2). The book of Alma emphasizes this order, contrasting the righteous order of the Son of God against the rival, wicked order of Nehors.[21] Alma invites disciples to "walk after the holy order of God" (Alma 7:22), giving us an entire chapter on what that looks like and means (see Alma 13). Today, the holy temple initiates us into this order and then teaches us the patterns to live according to this manner of righteous Saints. The temple is a modern school of prophets and prophetesses where we learn to live like Melchizedek (after whom the order was renamed because he was such a great high priest[22]), or enter into a covenant pattern to live like the Son of God. Living after the holy order includes such things as submitting to God's will by obedience, sacrificing for the greater good of the kingdom, living the higher law of Christ's teachings in His gospel, learning to control passion and power

THE HOLY COVENANTS

by being chaste, and building the kingdom of God through dedicated consecration and loving service.[23]

PRESENTING THE ORDER

The presentation of the temple endowment teaches these patterns of righteous living through an authorized, symbolic, covenant-making ceremony. Our washing and anointing in the temple initiates us into this holy way of living (thus, it is called "initiatory") and enables us to become clean and pure before God.[24] The initiatory illuminates our divine identity and potential and authorizes us to wear the temple garment.[25] The sacred temple garment we receive and wear under our clothing is a tangible, daily reminder that we are part of a priestly order and must live according to the holy covenants made as a representative of God's Son, whose name is upon us.

When we participate in the temple endowment ceremony, we experience and reenact[26] a symbolic upward journey that takes each one of us, as a fallen person, to being taught about the great plan of redemption, empowered by knowledge and covenants, and ultimately brought into the presence of God to become an heir of eternal life[27] (what the celestial room represents).[28] The ceremony suggests growth and progression from room to room, or glory to glory, as we increase in light and truth and make priesthood covenants to guide us in living a holy life. Following ancient patterns, the endowment presentation is a religious drama, or divine play, that reveals the hidden, sacred mysteries of God and His kingdom to the intimate covenant-initiated.[29] These principles are presented through symbolic characters, dialogue, signs, actions, and clothing.[30] Our priestly temple robes suggest our identity and future as a high priest or priestess.[31] In the Old Testament, the only people who were washed and anointed, put on priestly clothes, and entered the holiest room in the temple symbolizing God's presence were prophets, priests, and kings. Today, every worthy Latter-day Saint can do this, male and female. The Lord through His temple has indeed created a kingdom of priests.

While learning God's ways and making exalted priestly covenants is part of the "ancient order"[32] of things, how this ancient order and its associated covenants are presented in the temple has been adjusted over time by those with prophetic authority. Remember, there is a difference between endowment (the power and capacity to enter the presence of God[33] and receive a fulness of His exalted blessings) and the presentation of the endowment (a teaching tool). Words, actions, clothing,[34] setting, symbols, and other teaching methods can be authorized and adapted to communicate and bring the power of endowment in our lives.[35] We shouldn't presume to think that what we do in the temples today is exactly what Adam and Eve did, nor Abraham, Moses, or Solomon. Logically, it can't be. It isn't even exactly the same as it was when I began writing this book,[36] or even just a few decades ago, let alone centuries or millennia. If the endowment is the gift, the presentation of the endowment is the packaging to deliver the gift. The gift can be wrapped and delivered in various ways by God and His servants.[37]

GROWING IN THE ORDER

Unwrapping and utilizing this gift presented in the endowment ceremony takes time. Some things can be learned only through experience.[38] We must grow in degrees through time and practice to have our character molded by grace into the pattern of the Son of God. If we will live faithfully according to this holy order taught to us in the temple, eventually we will receive the fulness of God's priesthood (see D&C 124:28). We will receive "thrones, kingdoms, principalities, and powers, dominions" (D&C 132:19). Those thus exalted in the celestial kingdom from living after the holy covenant patterns will become "priests and kings [and priestesses and queens], who have received of his fulness . . . after the order of Melchizedek" (D&C 76:56–57).

Before we get too eternally excited, these exalted blessings are currently beyond our capacity. Most all of us are still figuring out the basics. I don't know about you, but I'm not ready to sit on eternal thrones and have angels subject to me (see D&C 132:20) when sometimes I struggle to sit in my car and subject my frustration with traffic. I have a lot of character growth to do. President John Taylor taught about this gap:

> We are all aiming at celestial glory. Don't you know we are? We are talking about it, and we talk about being kings and priests unto the Lord; we talk about being enthroned in the kingdoms of our God; we talk about being queens and priestesses; and we talk, when we get on our high-heeled shoes, about possessing thrones, principalities, powers, and dominions in the eternal worlds, when at the same time many of us do not know how to conduct ourselves any better than a donkey does. Notwithstanding our talk and our short comings, there is a reality in these things, and God is determined, if possible, to make something of us. In order to do this, he has to try us and prove us.[39]

THE HOLY COVENANTS

Since our baptism into the Church, we have learned and grown. We have shown some promise and been initiated into the modern school of the prophets, receiving the celestial teachings and covenants of the temple. Now, it's time to follow its order to become endowed with power. Metaphorically, we are like dedicated students who have been accepted to medical school and received their white coat, but we yet have many years of work and commitments to keep before we become competent physicians. Hear, therefore, the White Coat Parable.

THE WHITE COAT PARABLE

How does an ordinary girl find her way to becoming a doctor?

That was the question Regina James[1] wanted answered ever since she was young. Although she came from an average home, she was intelligent and driven, a potent combination that propelled her to academic success in high school and college, completing a challenging bachelor's degree in biophysics, and graduating magna cum laude. While an accomplishment in and of itself, it was merely a preparatory proving ground to meet the elevated requirements of medical school. She scored high on the MCAT—the medical college admissions test—and felt she had a good shot with a few of the medical schools where she had applied.

THE HOLY COVENANTS

Then, one day, sandwiched between ordinary emails was a message from Commerce Medical School. "Dear Ms. Regina James, the Medical College Admissions Committee has completed its review of applicants. We are most pleased to inform you that you have been accepted . . ."

Regina couldn't believe it. She called her mom and dad. They cried. Dr. James was on her way.

———

Her first day of medical school was doubly joyous and solemn, a formal meeting with all the newly accepted medical students and their families where a ritual would take place to launch them on their paths to becoming doctors. Known as the *white coat ceremony*, in solemnity medical students take the Hippocratic oath—a covenant[2] and promise of core principles to guide them throughout their professional lives.[3]

Regina sat, excited but unsure, and looked in the crowd for her parents to steady her while she waited.

Just then, the microphone crackled and the associate dean of the medical school spoke. "Welcome to your white coat ceremony, future doctors!" he said. The crowd applauded. The associate dean outlined the program. A pastor prayed. A soloist sang.

Then he announced, "We are now pleased to

have Dr. Snow, distinguished professor and Dean of Commerce Medical, administer our white coat ceremony."

Dean Snow rose to the lectern.

"Students, this is your official welcome to medical school. While you have shown promise, realize that you are at the beginning of a long professional journey to becoming actual physicians."

Her words were clear, direct, and powerful.

"To understand where you fit in the present, let's look a bit to the future," she said.

She then laid out a little of what was immediately ahead of the new medical students—a slew of science and anatomy courses, clinical clerkships and internships, four years to merely *prepare* for a medical residency, let alone any specialization. Regina felt overwhelmed already.

"Do you feel a bit intimidated?" the dean wryly asked, peering over her glasses to read their collective thoughts. "Good! You should. As I said, you are not doctors. Not yet. While we congratulate you on being found worthy and accepted to study, don't confuse capacity with ability. You have the first. You will spend a lifetime earning the second. You will grow in degrees, obtained by dedicated experience as you progress along the established path that countless doctors have previously followed."[4]

She continued, "To set you on this path, we ask each of you to make a solemn commitment to the practice. You are carrying a white coat in your arms that will soon be placed upon you by medical faculty who have already made and kept the same vows."

Tugging on the sleeve of her own white coat, the dean said, "These white coats are physical symbols of the values and responsibilities of medicine. Each time you don your coat, may you be reminded of the rights, responsibilities, privileges, and promises of the vocation of medicine—a tangible reminder of the lifelong obligations you are about to take upon you now."

She proceeded to call each individual student to come to the front, reciting their full names. Met by two other medical professors from the college, one by one, the students turned around, faced the audience, and had their white coats cloaked upon them.

Regina watched her classmates as they progressed through the alphabet until she heard, "Regina Phoebe James."

She stepped forward, turned, was coated, received a symbolic stethoscope and pin, shook hands, and was seated.

When each student had done likewise, the dean

said in a commanding voice, "All arise! In our profession, it is a custom established thousands of years ago that nobody may be admitted to its honors who has not first expressly undertaken its obligations. Now, therefore, I call upon you to take the oath of Hippocrates. Repeat after me:

"*I do solemnly swear by whatever each of us holds most sacred,*" she read.

The students repeated aloud, "*I do solemnly swear by whatever each of us holds most sacred.*"

"*That I will be loyal to the profession of medicine, and just and generous to its members.*"

A choral recitation of melded male and female voices followed, line after line and commitment after commitment.

"*That into whatsoever home I shall enter it shall be for the good of the sick and the well to the utmost of my power and that I will hold myself aloof from wrong and from corruption and from tempting others to vice.*

"*That I will exercise my art solely for the cure of my patients and the prevention of disease and will give no drugs and perform no operation for a criminal purpose and far less suggest such a thing.*

"*That whatsoever I shall see or hear of the lives of men and women which is not fitting to be spoke, I will keep inviolably secret.*

THE HOLY COVENANTS

"These things I do promise and in proportion as I am faithful to this oath, may happiness and good repute be ever mine, the opposite if I shall be forsworn.[5]

"*These things I do promise . . .*" the students concluded.

The dean paused, letting a few seconds' hesitation add gravity through silence.

"Thank you. You may be seated," she said. "You now have your white coat with your commitment to the principles and practices of the medical world. There is order and purpose to these—a higher calling to duty, commitment, service, selflessness, sacrifice, and compassion. These will advise you in changing circumstances when the decision to make or path to take isn't exactly clear."

Dr. Snow took one last, deep breath, exhaled, and concluded emphatically: "You have your white coats and all they symbolize; now go and grow into them, young physicians-in-training. The covenants you have made will help you fulfill the coat you are now privileged to wear."[6]

The dean sat down. The students applauded. The parents wept. Regina smiled. She wasn't there yet, and it would take years of being proven to fulfill her potential, but Dr. Regina James was on her way.

THE WHITE COAT PARABLE

Three years into medical school, Regina realized she was barely on her way. There was so much to learn, but she was excited to be learning it. She reveled in the textbooks, journal articles, labs, and professors that taught her clearly the truths and laws of the practice. Nobody was expected to know everything or be perfect, but to continue, you had to adhere to established criteria, which Regina did.

In her third year she began core clinical experiences, slowly gaining experience while working with professional physicians as mentors. One evening became embedded in her memory. Earlier that day, a young resident doctor had been attending a woman who had just come out of esophageal surgery. The intensive care unit needed to discharge a patient to make room for another. The resident doctor decided to trust his own judgment and disobeyed an established protocol, removing the breathing tube earlier than normal to transfer the woman. Suddenly, the woman's oxygen levels dropped. He tried to reinsert the breathing tube but couldn't. He quickly checked her airway and found her throat swollen shut. He finally succeeded, but the patient went over six minutes without oxygen.[7] Permanent brain damage was likely for the woman, all because established standards had not been obeyed. That evening, Regina's attending physician gathered all the students and solemnly reminded them, "There is no such thing as 'my way' medicine. Doing so leads to unnecessary pain and death."[8] That night reinforced to Regina her need to continually learn and gladly hearken to the regulations of the practice.

Now in her fourth year of school, Regina wore her white coat more comfortably, but medical school was anything but comfortable. This last year taxed Regina more than the previous three combined. Not in the intellectual expectations, but by the sacrifices that were required. Her fourth year necessitated the completion of her research and scholarly project, along with a focused internship with a supervised patient load, all while applying for a residency specialty. She knew this was to prepare her, as medical school curriculum builds progressively, but it was taking everything from her. Dating, free time, sleep, home-cooked meals, predictable schedules, relaxing Sundays—did nothing take higher priority? Year four seemed to test that question.

To her credit, Regina passed that test, and all her tests. After four years of medical school, she was officially "Dr. James" in title, but not yet in practice. She still had four years of residency ahead of her after being matched with a hospital to train her in her desired specialty. Dr. James was on her way to becoming a medical pathologist—a laboratory physician who studies blood and tissue to diagnose and manage disease. She felt it was a perfect path for her professional desires to research, diagnose, heal, and also teach.

Although Regina was excelling on paper, during residency she struggled somewhat in her demeanor. She sometimes lost patience with her patients. Her character was being tested as much as her knowledge or ability. Once when she was about to go home after a long shift, a man was checked in and needed a diagnosis. The senior attending physician turned to Regina.

"Dr. James, I need you to stay a bit longer and run these labs for Mr. Johnson."

Mr. Johnson was no stranger to the hospital, having been admitted many times due to issues related to his hard lifestyle.

Regina let out an unexpectedly unprofessional, "Are you serious?" the disdain evident in her tone alone. "I can diagnose him now. His liver is failing. Cirrhosis. Alcoholic liver disease. I don't even need a biopsy."

The senior physician pulled Regina to the side. "Dr. James," he said in a kind but corrective tone.

"I know, I know," she inserted. "I'll stay. Don't worry. But I'm just tired of trying to help someone like him who clearly doesn't want to help himself."

The senior physician pointedly responded, almost in a whisper: "Dr. James, you became a physician to care for people and work to heal them. You didn't become a physician to judge them. If you don't understand the difference, you have no right to train at this institution."[9]

The rebuke stung but was necessary to help shape her. There were many other experiences that taught Dr. Regina James that becoming an excellent physician required an exemplary character. The opportunity to become a physician required not just a capable mind, but a good heart also.

That character was required because her authority and capacity were growing. Lives were now in her hands, literally. She loved her increased ability to help so many, but she also was aware that a lapse in judgment could have grave consequences, for her and countless others who depended upon her. People trusted and respected her, and she knew she couldn't betray that confidence, despite pressures from certain hospital administrators, insurance companies, or unethical opportunities. Regina would hesitate to admit this, but once she and another resident sat during a lonely graveyard shift and hypothesized how a pathologist could go in with pharmaceutical companies to make serious money if tissues were consistently interpreted a certain way. It was a fleeting late-night conversation, but one that exposed how much power was in her hands, and why absolute integrity and trustworthiness were required. Dr. Regina James was committed to using that power ethically and not selfishly. She was choosing the right way.

⁓

After four years of residency and specialty clinicals, Dr. Regina James was hired as a medical pathologist for a cancer hospital connected to a research university. She had done it! Soon, Dr. James found herself mentoring and eventually overseeing other young medical students where she had been not too many years before, imparting wisdom and experience to help others gain the same. Once, a red-eyed medical student on a thirty-six-hour shift threw down his clipboard in exasperation and complained to her, "I'm so tired of that guy. This isn't what I signed up for."

"And just what *did* you think you were signing up for?" Dr. James asked him in return.

"Not being worked to the bone for years on end like this," he complained.

"Oh, I see," she said. "You wanted to gain pre-eminent knowledge and be endowed with extraordinary capacities the easy way, right? Take the quick, condensed, online course?" she asked with a smile.

"I wish. It's just taking everything I've got," the young med student admitted.

"It will take everything you've got. Becoming a physician is a complete, consecrated commitment," she said, emphasizing a hard *c* on all three words.

Tugging on his white coat, she said, "Isn't that what you signed up for, really, at your white coat ceremony? That type of commitment isn't casual, but it is ultimately what will qualify you to be worthy of those initials by your name."

―

A dozen years later, a young man named Jacob sat anxiously in a sea of unfamiliar faces. His eyes darted to the left and the right, leg bouncing in nervous excitement. He couldn't believe he was there and wasn't quite sure what lay ahead of him. Just then, there was a tap on the microphone.

Thump, thump, thump.

"Good morning, students, and welcome to your white coat ceremony. My name is Dr. Regina James, Associate Dean of the College of Medicine . . ."

Regina James had found her way.

THE WHY OF COVENANTS

Growing up, our family had this framed photo-collage that hung in our living room. It had a brown mat with dozens of various-sized and -shaped openings, filled with random but important photos: me in 1980s shorts, my parents on their wedding day, my sister as a baby. Individually the photos weren't much, but collectively they represented what was most important to my parents. The mat gave each photo its own space but placed it in the broader picture, taped down, secured, and bordered. That collaged mat had glass placed over it, and the glass was placed inside an oak frame that hung it all together to display safely on the wall. The photos could be seen but wouldn't be marked, hit, scratched, folded, or lost. The mat and frame acted to *connect* everything together, but also to *protect* it from harm.

Covenants do much of the same. They provide a framework by which we order our lives, connecting us to one another and to God through priesthood power. They also provide a way for us to secure God's promised blessings and protect us against forces that could destroy them. Priesthood covenants are like the frame around the picture of mortality that order, secure, bind, hold, and hang everything beautifully together. Priesthood covenants *connect* and *protect*.

TO CONNECT TO GOD

One of the primary reasons we make covenants with God is that they connect us directly to Him to become one with Him. As King Benjamin taught, "Because of the covenant which ye have made ye shall be called the children of Christ" (Mosiah 5:7), or we become known as the "covenant people of the Lord" (1 Nephi 14:14). Through baptism we "put on Christ," as Paul wrote (Galatians 3:27).

These covenants enable increased power from God. In some of the most important verses from the Restoration, the Lord teaches: "In the ordinances thereof [of the priesthood], the power of godliness is manifest. And without the ordinances thereof, and the authority of the priesthood, the power of godliness is not manifest unto men in the flesh" (D&C 84:20–21).

So, what "power of godliness" do the covenant ordinances of the Restoration give us? Here's one possible answer to consider for each ordinance:[1]

- Baptism = The purity and salvation of God
- The gift of the Holy Ghost = The mind and the heart (or character) of God
- Endowment = The knowledge, power, and capacity of God
- Sealing = The eternal increase and exaltation of God

There are other powers of godliness in these ordinances, of course, but the point is to see how the ability to become like God is directly tied to our covenant connection with Him.[2]

TO CONNECT TO EACH OTHER

Not only do covenants connect us to God, but they connect us to each other. Through faithful keeping of the covenant of eternal marriage made in the temple, my wife and I can be connected on earth and in heaven. Our children who are sealed to us can be eternally connected by the power of that priesthood covenant. I can be connected to my parents, and my wife to hers, and so forth. And through covenant, we are all connected into the priesthood family of God. When Joseph Smith was only seventeen years old, Moroni taught him that Elijah would restore to him priesthood so that "the promises made to the fathers" could become available (D&C 2:2). These promises are the exalted promises of Abraham ("the fathers") and the family sealing connections they offer,[3] without which this earth is "utterly wasted" (D&C 2:3), or pointless,[4] and would be "smitten with a curse" (D&C 128:18). The human family can and must be sealed up, welded together, matted and framed, connected by priesthood covenants with one another and with God.

TO PROTECT AGAINST SIN

We not only make covenants to connect to God and others, but we also make them to protect us against the adversary and ourselves. For example, there is covenant power in the Holy Ghost to warn of sin or discern falsehood, or in priesthood power to cast out, or in the temple garment to spiritually protect. But there is also a protective power in a covenant to remind and guide us, to bind and hold us, and to stabilize and moralize us. Touching on covenants, author David Brooks wrote, "Commitment is falling in love with something and then building a structure of

THE WHY OF COVENANTS

behaviour around it for the moment when love falters."[5] Although my wife and I deeply love each other, it is likely that had we not made a covenant commitment to bind ourselves to one another twenty-four years ago (as of the writing of this book), we might not be together today. Something could have more easily got in our way: another man or woman, career ambitions, personal preferences, self-actualization, disagreements, health, finances, or more. Without the structure of covenant commitment, it becomes increasingly difficult to hold love together against forces that, like entropy, naturally want to tear it apart.

The purpose of this isn't to write about marriage, but to use marriage and love to illustrate why we make covenants on a broader whole with the God that we love. We commit to God by covenant now knowing that moments of weakness will come that may tempt us later. Elder Dale G. Renlund and Sister Ruth L. Renlund wrote that "covenants are pledges or vows that guarantee the future behavior of the participant."[6] When we make covenants of chastity or obedience or consecration in the temple, we aren't covenanting only what we will do that day of the year, but what we will do in *future days and years*. Our covenants protect us against a tempted version of ourselves. As an example, I once felt a prompting that a demanding Church calling was soon coming my way. To be honest, I didn't want it. But while my initial reaction was to reject it, my prior covenant commitment of consecration helped rectify and straighten me in my moment of spiritual instability, and I accepted the calling when it was extended. Covenants act as guideposts when vision becomes clouded.

Thus, the professional athlete and motivational Christian speaker Tim Tebow says that we shouldn't listen to our *emotions*, but to our *convictions*.[7] C. S. Lewis said that once we commit to Christ there will come a time when our "emotions will rise up and carry out a blitz on [our] belief," so we must learn to "teach [our] moods 'where they get off'" if we are even to be "a sound Christian."[8] Read how the Anti-Nephi-Lehis were corrected by their covenant in a moment of logical, rational, understandable, and even compassionate desire to act against their earlier commitments (see Alma 53:10–17). As Robert Robinson expressed in the beautiful hymn "Come, Thou Fount of Every Blessing," we are

> *Prone to wander, Lord, I feel it;*
> *Prone to leave the God I love;*
> *Here's my heart, O take and seal it;*
> *Seal it for thy courts above.*

THE WHY OF COVENANTS

Covenants bind and seal us to righteous patterns of behavior precisely because our later desires may betray us. They protect us against our own instability.

HOPE THROUGH COVENANTS

Because covenants connect us and protect us, they give us hope that we can inherit God's promised blessings, grace, and priesthood power. The author of Hebrews wrote that we should "shew the same diligence to the full assurance of hope . . . Who through faith and patience inherit the promises" (Hebrews 6:11–12). President Dieter F. Uchtdorf taught, "Hope is . . . the abiding trust that the Lord will fulfill His promise to us. It is confidence that if we live according to God's laws and the words of His prophets now, we will receive desired blessings in the future."[9]

Yes, in covenants we make promises, but never forget that God does also, and His promises are sure. He promises us that if we will become covenant Saints through the ordinances of the priesthood, He will connect us, protect us, redeem us, and exalt us (see D&C 84:35–41). The only question that remains is whether we will enter into and live the covenants to secure those blessings offered through the holy priesthood in His restored Church.

THE HOLY COVENANTS

COVENANTS = THE RESTORED CHURCH

Overall, the Restoration of the Church is all about the restoration of these covenants of salvation and exaltation.[10] There are many churches that teach about Jesus. There are many churches that do good. There are many churches that provide a sense of community. Some of them may even do these things better than us. We love, respect, and work together with them. But humbly we also proclaim that no other church on the earth offers the authorized priesthood covenants of salvation and exaltation. This was the message from *day one* of this work. When the Lord appeared to a fourteen-year-old Joseph Smith, He told him many things, but central to the things Joseph learned was "that the Everlasting covena[n]t was broken."[11] When the Church was organized in April 1830, the Lord summarized the entire reason for the Church was so that the covenant could be reestablished (see D&C 22). The covenant had died, and the Restoration was here to resurrect it.

Nephi wrote of the Restoration: "The Lord God will proceed to do a marvelous work . . . *unto the making known of the covenants of the Father of heaven unto Abraham.* . . . Wherefore, the Lord God will proceed to make bare his arm in the eyes of all the nations, in bringing about *his covenants and his gospel*" (1 Nephi 22:8–9, 11; emphasis added).

We are COVENANT Saints. That sets us apart and is another level from being BELIEVING Saints. The Lord Himself said, "Ye are the children of the prophets; and ye are of the house of Israel; and ye are of the covenant which the Father made with your fathers, saying unto Abraham: And in thy seed shall all the kindreds of the earth be blessed . . . and this because ye are the children of the covenant" (3 Nephi 20:25–26).

THE COVENANTS OF ABRAHAM

When people are baptized into the authorized Church, they become part of the covenant house of Israel. They are numbered as His people, counted as His sheep, and receive the promised blessings of celestial *salvation* (to be with God in heaven). When covenant members of the house of Israel enter the holy temple to participate in its ordinances, they make further covenants with God to receive the blessings of celestial *exaltation* (to become like God in heaven).

Sometimes we call the covenants of exaltation the "Abrahamic covenant." Abraham is one of the main prophets and patriarchs of the Old Testament, the father of Isaac and Jacob (later renamed Israel). The scriptures teach us that Abraham "became a rightful heir, a High Priest" (Abraham 1:2). An heir of what? An heir of the blessings of exaltation. Sometimes these eternal blessings of exaltation are broken down into three "Ps" (see Abraham 2:6, 8–10):

- Promised land
  (inherit the celestial kingdom)
- Priesthood
  (receive heavenly authority and power)
- Posterity
  (obtain eternal marriage and increase)

Although it is commonly known as the "Abrahamic Covenant," this isn't Abraham's covenant any more than it's Melchizedek's priesthood. These are the covenants and promises of exaltation, and these covenant promises started with Adam and Eve (see Abraham 1:3).

When we got baptized, we became part of this covenant family, and thus became potential heirs of the same eternal blessings they were promised. Through the covenants of the temple we can advance to one day become rightful heirs, like Abraham or Sarah, of all the blessings of exaltation. Covenant connection enables our eternal perfection.

THE WHY OF COVENANTS

THE ENDOWMENT COVENANTS

Thus, to receive a fulness of the promises, power, and priesthood of God, we must enter into the holy order of God through temple ordinances and covenants. "Let [a] house be built unto my name, that I may reveal mine ordinances therein unto my people" (D&C 124:40). An ordinance is an authorized religious ceremony, done under the direction and authority of the priesthood.[12] Ordinances that are needed for salvation and exaltation are accompanied by a covenant, or a promise, between the participant and God.[13] In the ordinances of the temple we make several covenants to help us learn how to live a holy life patterned after Jesus Christ.

Elder Robert D. Hales of the Quorum of the Twelve Apostles taught that in the temple:

> We establish patterns of Christlike living. These include obedience, making sacrifices to keep the commandments, loving one another, being chaste in thought and action, and giving of ourselves to build the kingdom of God. Through the Savior's Atonement and by following these basic patterns of faithfulness, we receive "power from on high" to face the challenges of life. We need this divine power today more than ever. It

is power we receive only through temple ordinances.[14]

Although some are unaware, these temple covenants have been discussed and published publicly numerous times.[15] Elder David A. Bednar said, "Across the generations, from the Prophet Joseph Smith to President Russell M. Nelson, the doctrinal purposes of temple ordinances and covenants have been taught extensively by Church leaders," including covenants such as "the law of obedience, the law of sacrifice, the law of the gospel, the law of chastity, and the law of consecration."[16] The Church has recently published a website with "Prophetic Teachings on the Temple,"[17] with some references to the major ceremonies and covenants of the temple, which everyone should read and study. It has also published a summary of the endowment ceremony along with brief definitions of the five major temple covenants in the *General Handbook* for all members.[18]

The chapters that follow in this book suggest some ways to understand those covenants and live them in our everyday lives. These major temple covenants and chapters include:

- To live the law of obedience (or law of the Lord)

THE WHY OF COVENANTS

- To live the law of sacrifice
- To live the law of the gospel
- To live the law of chastity
- To live the law of consecration

Related to these covenants, two chapters will also discuss the obligations to not disclose sacred teachings of the temple and to wear the temple garment faithfully.[19] To grasp these commitments, let us look at an *explanation* (what), an *application* (how), and a *motivation* (why) for each temple covenant to help us become more fully endowed with spiritual power in our daily lives.

PART II
THE COVENANTS

"If a man gets the fulness of God he has to get in the same way that Jesus Christ obtained it & that was by keeping all the ordinances of the house of the Lord."

—JOSEPH SMITH

THE COMMITMENT TO WEAR THE GARMENT

As part of the initiatory ordinance, we are authorized and covenant[1] to wear the sacred temple garment under our clothing to serve as a physical symbol and spiritual reminder of our desire to live a holier life.[2] These garments of the Holy Priesthood,[3] as they are sometimes called, are deeply significant and symbolic. As part of a 2019 letter on preparing for the temple, the First Presidency wrote:

> The temple garment is a reminder of covenants made in the temple and, when worn properly throughout life, will serve as a protection against temptation and evil. The garment should be worn beneath the outer clothing. It should not be removed for activities that can

reasonably be done while wearing the garment, and it should not be modified to accommodate different styles of clothing. Endowed members should seek the guidance of the Holy Spirit to answer personal questions about wearing the garment.[4]

Like many things related to the Church and temple, for some, wearing the temple garment is very sacred and meaningful, for others it is routine and expected, and for others it feels inhibiting or unnecessary. Regardless of personal views, it is so important to wear that one of the questions to maintain a current temple recommend is, "Do you keep the covenants that you made in the temple, including wearing the temple garment as instructed in the endowment?"[5] Why is the covenant to wear this underclothing so spiritually significant? If we understand what the temple garment seeks to do doctrinally, it can help us better answer what to do with it practically.

AN EXPLANATION: PRIESTLY COVENANTS

Sacred, special religious clothing is mentioned in the scriptures many times. One of my favorites is in the law of Moses, when the children of Israel were told to make "fringes in the borders of their garments throughout their generations" of a "ribband of blue"

THE COMMITMENT TO WEAR THE GARMENT

(Numbers 15:38). Why have a blue ribbon on their clothes? The Lord said it is so "that ye may look upon it [the blue ribbon], and remember all the commandments of the Lord, and do them" (v. 39). Our temple garments also have embroidered threads in them, or several simple marks that serve as a reminder of our covenants to God.[6] I served my two-year Church mission in an area where no temple was accessible for missionaries. I was grateful that even without being able to participate in temple ceremonies for so long, I could personally remember and find power in temple covenants as I got dressed by mentally rehearsing what the garment symbolized related to my sacred temple commitments.

The scriptures speak of special clothing for those who were to be priests for God. Exodus 28 discusses how Aaron and other temple priests should have "holy garments" (v. 2) made for them, including "linen breeches to cover their nakedness; from the loins even unto the thighs" (v. 42). "And thou shalt bring Aaron and his sons unto the door of the tabernacle of the congregation, and wash them with water. And thou shalt put upon Aaron the holy garments, and anoint him, and sanctify him; that he may minister unto me in the priest's office" (Exodus 40:12–13). Remember that we are to become, one day, great high priestesses or priests. Our temple garment is a reminder of that promised potential and the covenants with which we should comply to attain those exalted blessings. In some other faiths, ordained priests wear a collar or special outer clothing to signify their dedication to God. We also have been initiated into a priestly way of life, and our temple garment symbolizes this sacred call. The difference is that our priestly clothing is worn as an underlayer instead of an outer one.[7] Sister Linda S. Reeves of the Relief Society General Presidency summarized that through "the proper wearing of our temple garment," she is "symbolically putting on *royal robes* given me by my Heavenly Father."[8]

AN APPLICATION: TO PROVIDE PROTECTION AND FOSTER MODESTY

There seem to be two basic, practical purposes for wearing the temple garment:

1. To provide protection
2. To foster modesty

In his book *The Holy Temple*, President Boyd K. Packer wrote that "The garment . . . becomes a shield and protection to the wearer."[9] The temple garment has been repeatedly discussed as a type of armor of God.[10] This metaphor and protective promise is sometimes interpreted as something physical. While this may be true in some instances, never forget that the greatest protection we seek is spiritual, for "we wrestle not against flesh and blood" but "against spiritual wickedness" (Ephesians 6:12). Our highest aim is to live a holy way of life, not to merely avoid physical pain in life. The Church teaches that the temple garment provides protection for the wearer against temptation and evil.[11] We shouldn't diminish experiences we have when the garment provides physical protection, but the spiritual protection it offers seems to be much more broadly applicable and consistently emphasized. This protection is conditional upon our faithfulness in keeping our covenants.[12]

Although the overall significance of the garment is much deeper, promoting chastity and modesty is another practical aspect of the garment.[13] In 1988 the First Presidency explained, "The principles of modesty and keeping the body appropriately covered are implicit in the covenant and should govern the nature of all clothing worn."[14] Respecting the private parts of our bodies and conducting ourselves in moral decency are essential elements of living a holy life after the order of the Son of God. The temple garment can help facilitate this behavior.

We would do well, however, to remember that

modesty in clothing can be a relative idea. What is modest to one person and culture can be immodest to another, and vice versa. For example, President Brigham Young once lamented about the latest immodest dresses that Latter-day Saint women were wearing that were *too long*, dragging in the streets and getting dirty. Brigham asked them to make their dresses *shorter* to be more modest. But, he pled, "Do not be extravagant and cut them so short that we can see the tops of your stockings."[15] Not the tops of our stockings! Today, both those definitions of immodesty have faded from most modern cultures.

My reason for relating this cultural modesty relativism is so that we don't abuse the garment by weaponizing it as a judgmental marker against others. Some people scroll social media feeds and see Church member Dave on vacation or Jenny in her workout clothes and their first thought is, "Is he/she wearing their temple garments?" There are a number of factors that affect why and how someone wears the temple garment—some practical and others understandably private. Like Sabbath day observance, let our wearing of the garment be a personal sign[16] we send to God of our covenant commitments, but let's avoid pharisaical measurements of others' short lengths and shoulder exposures.

THE COMMITMENT TO WEAR THE GARMENT

A MOTIVATION: TO TAKE UPON THE NAME OF CHRIST

Perhaps most significantly, the temple garment is a tactile symbol of our Lord's redemptive sacrifice. In the holy temple we more fully take upon ourselves the name of Christ,[17] and in wearing the temple garment, in a way, we quite literally do so. In the Garden of Eden, Adam and Eve found themselves naked, hiding from God due to their shame (see Genesis 3:9–10). *Naked* is a term often used to denote feeling embarrassed or unprepared. John the Revelator tapped into this concept when he wrote of Jesus's return: "Behold, I come as a thief. Blessed [is] he that watcheth, and keepeth his garments, lest he walk naked, and they see his shame" (Revelation 16:15). The Book of Mormon prophet Jacob taught that at the Judgment, "We shall have a perfect knowledge of all our guilt, and our uncleanness, and our nakedness" (2 Nephi 9:14). In our mortal weakness, we want and need something to cover our sins, or our nakedness.

Jesus made coats of skins (likely from sacrificial animals) for Adam and Eve to cover their nakedness (see Genesis 3:21). This is deeply symbolic of our Lord's own sacrifice to cover, cleanse, protect, and redeem from sin through His Atonement. President

THE HOLY COVENANTS

Russell M. Nelson wrote, "Rich meaning is found in study of the word 'atonement' in the Semitic languages of Old Testament times. In Hebrew, the basic word for atonement is *kaphar*, a verb that means 'to cover' or 'to forgive.'"[18]

The scriptures testify that the righteous will also be "clothed upon" by Jesus (D&C 29:13; D&C 109:76). The Apostle Paul comforted us by saying: "Being clothed [by Christ] we shall not be found naked" (2 Corinthians 5:3) at the judgment bar. Those who have taken upon themselves the name of Christ by covenant are the ones whose nakedness will be covered with the "robe of righteousness" (2 Nephi 9:14), or with the "garments of salvation" (Isaiah 61:10). Our temple garment is a physical and literal reminder of our spiritual covenant that Christ's name is upon us. When we put on the garment, we "put on Christ" (Galatians 3:27), and therefore the blessings of His infinite Atonement.

To those who understand the deeper spiritual significance of temple garments, they become "beautiful garments" (Isaiah 52:1), "garments of salvation" (Isaiah 61:10), "holy garments" (Exodus 28:2), and something to be treasured. The temple garment reminds us on a daily basis that we have connection and protection in covenants; it represents Jesus and His Atonement covering our nakedness from sin; it

THE COMMITMENT TO WEAR THE GARMENT

is a piece of the temple we can always take and have with us to empower us. Faithfully wearing the garment becomes our symbol of priestly covenant connection with God, protecting, reminding, and fostering patterns of holiness. With the view of Christ as our spiritual bridegroom, the parable of the wedding garment told by Jesus takes on added meaning: "And when the king came in to see the guests, he saw there a man which had not on a wedding garment. . . . Then said the king to the servants, Bind him hand and foot, and take him away . . . For many are called, but few are chosen" (Matthew 22:11, 13).

THE PROMISE TO NOT REVEAL SACRED TEACHINGS

It is well known that in the holy temple we learn sacred teachings that are not to be disclosed outside of its walls, and some things only at certain places even within its walls. There are various examples from scripture of times when the Lord restricted certain information from being discussed publicly, such as on the Mount of Transfiguration (see Matthew 17:9), or after the brother of Jared's visions (see Ether 3:21), or after the Lord prayed with the Nephites (see 3 Nephi 19:32–34). From the beginning, Joseph Smith followed the same pattern, saying that there were certain things to be had only in sacred settings. On May 1, 1842, he preached a sermon about the temple, explaining: "The keys are certain signs & words by which false

THE PROMISE TO NOT REVEAL SACRED TEACHINGS

spirits & personages may be detected from true.—which cannot be revealed to the Elders till the Temple is completed."[1] When Heber C. Kimball received some of this sacred temple knowledge, he wrote a letter to Parley P. Pratt, who was in England, telling him that he had received sacred teachings from Joseph but that he couldn't commit them in writing in a letter—Parley had to come get them for himself.[2]

While the temple itself states very clearly that specific aspects should not be publicly disclosed, there remains confusion over what we can and can't say generally about what goes on related to the temple endowment. Perhaps as you read parts of this book you might worry or think, "Should he write about *that*?" It's an important question, as one of the covenants we make in the temple is to not disclose certain sacred teachings from the temple endowment ceremony.

AN EXPLANATION: WHAT'S BEEN SAID ABOUT WHAT CAN BE SAID?

I've significantly researched the question of what can and can't appropriately be discussed about the temple. What I have found is that from the beginning, Church leaders have been open to discussing the overall purposes of the endowment. They repeatedly discuss the major covenants. They explain that the endowment teaches the plan of salvation. Some have openly used temple-specific phrases.[3] Individual Church leaders do seem to vary, however, in how much they're personally inclined to publicly teach or say.

In general, various statements from Church leaders advise us to not be too casual when talking about the temple endowment and to avoid discussing sacred aspects and words[4] of the ceremonies "in detail."[5] We can talk about the interior of the temple and our feelings about it.[6] More recently there has been encouragement to talk about the covenants of the temple, particularly before someone is entering for the first time—a welcome sign for this book![7] While these general guidelines can help, they sometimes leave members yet wondering where to draw boundaries about discussing the endowment.

AN APPLICATION: GUIDELINES TO DISCUSSING THE ENDOWMENT

Thus, as Elder David A. Bednar said, "Many Church members are unsure about what appropriately can and cannot be said regarding the temple experience outside of the temple." Related to that, he gave perhaps two of the clearest and most recent guidelines

THE PROMISE TO NOT REVEAL SACRED TEACHINGS

given, one for what we CAN talk about, the other for what we CAN'T:

- **CAN:** We may discuss the basic purposes of and the doctrine and principles associated with temple ordinances and covenants.
- **CAN'T:** We should not disclose or describe the special symbols associated with the covenants we receive in sacred temple ceremonies. Neither should we discuss the holy information that we specifically promise in the temple not to reveal.[8]

Taken collectively from Church leaders, Church curriculum, and the temple itself, four questions we can ask ourselves to help us know how to keep our covenant to maintain the sacred things of the temple are these:

1. Did I make a covenant in the temple to not discuss *this* outside of the temple or to only share it at a specific place in the temple?
2. Do Church leaders publicly discuss it, or is it found in Church literature and publications?
3. Is it found and discussed in the scriptures?

4. If it can be discussed, am I doing so appropriately and in the right setting?

For example, can we discuss that we learn through a video presentation[9] in the endowment ceremony about the plan of salvation, the Creation, the Fall, and redemption by Christ's Atonement? I hope so, as I just wrote that! How can I feel confident with that disclosure? Following the four guidelines:

1. We do not make a covenant to not discuss those truths.
2. There are multiple Church leaders and sources who have discussed this. (Here's just one example: "The plan of salvation is presented [in the endowment], including the Creation of the world, the Fall of Adam and Eve, the Atonement of Jesus Christ, the Apostasy, and the Restoration."[10])
3. These doctrinal concepts are repeatedly taught in the scriptures (see Genesis 1–4, Moses 2–5).
4. The way I phrased it is respectful, general, and in an appropriate setting—a carefully reviewed book that will mostly be read by temple-minded Latter-day Saints.

THE PROMISE TO NOT REVEAL SACRED TEACHINGS

These guidelines are not foolproof, of course, and we must always let wisdom and the Spirit guide, but they have proven helpful for me in striving to balance the delicate line of what should be responsibly discussed and what is under covenant to remain private.

A MOTIVATION: THE CHARACTER OF CONFIDENCES

Reflecting on this *nondisclosure* question in the light of the broader concept of developing holy patterns of living, however, reveals a deeper principle than mere privacy: it is the ability to develop a character of confidences. Some of the principles of godhood are about becoming a trustworthy person; someone who can keep privacies, can exercise discretion, and has self-control. Someone who knows what is not fitting to speak about publicly and can keep it inviolably secret. Joseph Smith once said he could keep something private until "doomsday" if needed, saying, "The reason we do not have the secrets of the Lord revealed unto us, is because we do not keep them, but reveal them."[11]

If the Lord is going to reveal unto us His reserved mysteries for the faithful, then keeping covenants to not reveal special symbols and specific teachings from the temple ceremony reflects our readiness in character, maturity, and spirituality to receive those "hidden things, which no man knew" that are "most precious" (D&C 101:33); those things that the Lord "delights" to reveal "to those who serve me in righteousness and in truth unto the end"(D&C 76:5).

Let us follow the guidelines given about what can and can't be discussed to keep our covenant to not reveal certain sacred temple teachings. Let us see this covenant, however, in a bigger picture related to developing Christlike character—one that can be trusted, is temperate with self-control, and can exercise prudence and confidence with sacred information. Because, "to them," the Lord says, "will I reveal all mysteries, yea, all the hidden mysteries of my kingdom from days of old, and for ages to come. . . . Yea, even the wonders of eternity shall they know, and things to come will I show them. . . . And their wisdom shall be great, and their understanding reach to heaven" (D&C 76:6–9).

THE LAW OF OBEDIENCE

It's been said that obedience is the first law of heaven.[1] It is also the first of the five major covenants that we make in the temple.[2] Indeed, the Lord summarized one of the entire purposes of mortality as our choosing to do all things that He commands (see Abraham 3:25). Obeying the law of God, or the law of the Lord as it is sometimes called, means that we learn the directives of God, submit to them, and strive to follow them.[3] Those divine directives are found in scriptures and in the words of living prophets.

Brigham Young asked:

> Will the Latter-day Saints observe the law of the Lord? If they will, it is all I ask of them. You can read the law of the Lord for yourselves

in the Old and New Testaments, in the Book of Mormon, and in the Book of Revelations given for this Church through Joseph the Prophet.[4]

AN EXPLANATION: SUBMISSION TO THE LIVING LAW

In a very broad sense, *a law* of the Lord is any policy, rule, expectation, direction, obligation, practice, or command given by God or His authorized servants to His Saints.[5] Obedience to *the* law of the Lord is following directives we receive from Jesus, because, as He tells us, "Behold, I am the law" (3 Nephi 15:9).

When we hear the word *obedience* related to this covenant, we may be tempted to associate it with people who do everything precisely as they are told or don't ever make mistakes. For mere mortals like you and me, that is a problematic definition. How can we keep the sacred covenant of obedience if we are sometimes, well, human? Perhaps looking at obedience through another lens may prove helpful. The root word for *obedience* suggests submission,[6] not flawlessness. Being faithful derives from deep loyalty, not absolute purity.[7] The etymology of "keeping" something (like commandments) originates from words like *desire*, *look out for*, and *persist* as much as putting into practice.[8] Simply put, to be obedient means we submit to be loyal and persist in trying to follow Christ.

Because the law is a person (Jesus), our submission is to be obedient to the LORD and not to some independent set of rules. This is an important point to understand, as what Jesus directs at one time may not be what He directs at another. At the height of the COVID-19 pandemic, I was struck by the irony of a sign posted at my local bank requiring masks to be worn to do business, posted right next to a pre-2020 sign that hadn't yet been removed requiring customers to remove anything covering their face, eyes, or head. A complete rule reversal! This is because some requirements are driven by circumstances. Just like how government laws sometimes change depending on the conditions of society, sometimes the laws of God can also change based on the conditions of His children. The Old Testament law is perhaps the most obvious example. Although we call it the law of Moses, it was delivered by Jehovah, the Lord, the Lawgiver (see 3 Nephi 15:5). The law of Moses contained hundreds of commands, including laws about offering animal sacrifices, ritual purity, stoning adulterers, and required annual feasts, none of which we obey today. This law was fulfilled by Christ with His new covenant during His ministry (see 3 Nephi 15:1–9). Although this law of Moses was replaced, it was the binding law of God to His covenant people for well over a thousand years, and the standard to which they were held accountable for that time.

While certain laws or commandments persist across dispensations, like chastity or obedience,[9] some laws of God continue to change, even in our dispensation. Saints in the 1800s were commanded to gather physically to Zion as part of the law of the Lord.[10] Others were asked to live with all things common or with stewardship of properties.[11] The Word of Wisdom originally was not a commandment, but merely wise counsel (see D&C 89:2). Today, for us, it's a binding law.[12] The law of tithing was originally ten percent of our income *plus* all of our "surplus property"[13] (see D&C 119:1, 4). Plural marriage was at one time part of the law of God (see D&C 132:32); now it's directly stated to be against it.[14] Like building codes for a home, we are held to the *current* laws of God, not past ones that have been supplanted, nor future ones that may one day be established by the voice of God.

AN APPLICATION: THE MODERN LAW OF GOD

So, what is the current law of the Lord? One place to find it is in Doctrine and Covenants 42. In late 1830, the Lord directed members of His Church in

THE LAW OF OBEDIENCE

the east to leave their homes and farms to gather and live with Saints in Ohio. He promised them that if they would make this enormous sacrifice, then when they got there He would endow them with power (see D&C 38:30). Connected to that, He said He would "give unto [them] my law" (D&C 38:32). In Doctrine and Covenants 42, the Lord begins, "Hearken and hear and obey the law which I shall give unto you" (v. 1). He proceeds to lay out two dozen or so "thou shalt" or "thou wilt" or "ye shall" commands. They include standard societal laws like "thou shalt not kill" (see v. 18) but also family-centered laws like "thou shalt love thy [spouse] with all thy heart" (v. 22). We should study and know Doctrine and Covenants 42 in our desire to obey the law of God and be endowed with power, as it continues to act as a law for the Church today.[15]

We would also do well to read the teachings in the *General Handbook* (published publicly to all) to be informed of the policies, practices, expectations, and duties of current Church members as set forth by the First Presidency and Twelve Apostles.[16] We would be benefited to study and know priesthood duties[17] set out therein, expectations on tithing,[18] the Word of Wisdom, Sabbath-day worship, and other directives that could influence our ability to attend the temple or be faithful covenant members of the Church. We should also listen to or read prophetic talks, letters, and declarations to learn the current law of the Lord.[19]

A MOTIVATION: TERRIBLY OBEDIENT

Years ago, I took my fifteen-year-old daughter out to drive for the first time so she could earn her learner's permit. It was a harrowing experience, to say the least. When we got in the car, her first question was what "PRNDL" meant. She then asked which pedal the brake was and which was the gas. I told her I'd answer her questions, but I first needed to pray. With her first left turn, she turned onto the opposite side of the road into oncoming traffic. She went too fast on turns and too slow on straightaways. She didn't yield at a roundabout. But, to her credit, she was trying. She was desiring. She was persisting. She didn't do everything perfectly, and I didn't expect her to. But she tried to listen and learn what she should do, fixing it when she didn't. She was a terribly obedient driver, in every sense of the phrase. You can connect the analogy.

Let's remember that part of obedience to the Lord's law is to keep the commandment to repent (see 3 Nephi 27:20; D&C 19:15). Being an "obedient sinner" is not an oxymoron. Obedience is *alignment* with God's will. Surely, doing right and avoiding sin is one of the ways we show Jesus we love and are loyal to Him (see John 14:15), but so is repentance, which is why He loves a repentant heart so much (see Luke 15:7). The temple law of obedience isn't the law of perfection or mistake-free living. This is important to remember as we learn—sometimes through failure—to live the holy order and ways of the Son of God. The Lord understands that we have shortcomings to work through, with His help. If we persist, gradually our ability to implement the law will increase. If our desire is to learn and hearken to His word, we will align and realign (or repent) each time we fall short, and we are on our way to keeping this covenant. We can obey the law of God in weakness.

In the end, keeping our covenant to live the law of God implies an inner disposition to do what God directs and an aspiration to have the law of God written in our hearts.[20] Like Ezra, let us "seek the law of the Lord, and to do it, and to teach in Israel statutes and judgments" (Ezra 7:10), helping ourselves and others avoid unnecessary pain and spiritual death. As Joseph Smith wrote of the Saints in 1831 who first received Doctrine and Covenants 42, let us receive the Lord's law "gladly."[21] The Lord will continue to give His laws and commands to His children who desire to learn, listen, align, and strive to loyally obey. He has promised to endow those who do with power, and as Joseph Smith said, "will bring all his subjects, who have obeyed his voice and kept his commandments, into his celestial rest."[22]

THE LAW OF SACRIFICE

Part of living after the covenant holy order or pattern of the Son of God is learning to develop the same spirit of sacrifice exemplified by our Lord. The law of sacrifice is to willingly give up what God asks us to let go of in order to build the kingdom of God, giving our lives to do so. In the holy temple we covenant to live this law of sacrifice.

From the beginning, holy women and men have manifested this willingness to give up what God asks them to let go. The first sacrifice in the covenant mortal story is when Eve and Adam sacrificed a state of paradise to move the plan of God forward. Even after that, God continued to call upon them to develop a spirit of sacrifice, commanding Adam and Eve to take the firstborn of their flocks and "offer sacrifices unto the Lord" as a form of worshipping Him (Moses 5:4–6). To help our first parents understand why, they were taught: "This thing is a similitude of the sacrifice of the Only Begotten of the Father. Wherefore, thou shalt do all that thou doest in the name of the Son" (Moses 5:7–8). "This thing" can be read as meaning that the sacrifice of their firstborn animals foreshadowed Jesus's sacrifice of His life. But "this thing" can also mean what must go on inside of us—learning to have a heart willing to let go of everything for God, just like Jesus. In this sense, even though sacrificing animals ended after Jesus gave His life on the cross, the internal law of sacrifice has never gone away. Everyone, from the beginning until now, has had to learn to give up what God asks them to let go.

AN EXPLANATION: LAYING DOWN OUR LIVES

We sometimes talk of laying down our lives for the gospel and kingdom as the ultimate sacrifice as though we might be killed as martyrs, which some have sadly done, and others may yet do. But for the great majority of us who will never suffer such a fate, laying down our lives for the kingdom has more to do with laying down our natural man than it does laying down our natural lives. The natural man—the selfishness, pride,

THE LAW OF SACRIFICE

power, praise, lust, grudge, envy, and the like—is what gets in our way of becoming like God and building His kingdom. To lay down our lives is to give up the unholy parts of our nature so that one day we can be qualified to rule and reign as kings and queens in God's kingdom. Only in losing our ungodly lives do we find our eternal ones (see Matthew 10:39).

Thus, like a progressive order, learning to first submit and obey the law of God helps prepare us to live the law of sacrifice.[1] One of the reasons God asks us to sacrifice is to make manifest what we truly love[2] (see John 15:13). Does nothing take higher priority than God? The law of sacrifice tests that question. He wants to reveal what's really in our hearts, and nothing cuts to the heart of true priorities like asking someone to give something up. Abraham, do you love me more than your son? Sariah, do you love my commands more than you love your comforts? Colesville Saints, do you love the New Jerusalem more than you love your new farms? Martin, do you love my word more than you love your wealth? Jessica, do you love my celestial requirements more than you love your social reputation? Sacrifice cuts through vain words and rote actions to lay bare what we really prioritize.

THE HOLY COVENANTS

AN APPLICATION: FOUR WAYS TO SACRIFICE

To live the covenant of laying down our lives for the kingdom, there seem to be four practical things all Saints can do:

1. Offer up a broken heart and a contrite spirit to God.
2. Keep the commandments of God.
3. Implement prophetic directives.
4. Follow personal direction from the Spirit.

First, as has been mentioned, we all must sacrifice our natural-man tendencies that are contrary to God's character (see Mosiah 3:19), offering up a broken heart and contrite spirit,[3] as Jesus taught us to do to live this law (see 3 Nephi 9:20). That phrase, a "broken heart and a contrite spirit," signifies that we are willing to yield to God, to humbly let Him prevail and rule in our lives,[4] to faithfully say, "Not my will, but thine be done," as Jesus showed.

What we are really sacrificing is our prideful, self-directed will and offering instead a meek, God-instructed one. Ironically, everything else we are asked to ever give up—in terms of temporal things of this earth—don't even originate with us in the first place. All we have, down to our very breath and mortal lives, are gifts from God (see Mosiah 2:21–23). The only thing that may be truly ours to give up is our will.[5]

With this humbled heart, we are willing and ready to keep His declared commandments, follow His authorized prophets, and listen to His holy Spirit. Those are three different things, from general to specific. Timeless commandments such as not lying, killing, nor committing adultery, and loving, forgiving, and serving others are for all; timely prophetic directives, such as paying tithing or serving missions or taking names to the temple, are global but usually pertain to current Saints who have made covenants with Christ; and Spirit-directed promptings that call for personal sacrifices will align with commandments and prophetic directives but are often individual and not generalizable—quit listening to that music or watching that show, give up this behavior on the Sabbath, spend more of your time with this family member, let go of those personal plans for these better ones God has for you.

A MOTIVATION: SACRIFICE AND REWARD

Whether through specific promptings, prophetic directives, or general commandments, God will ask all of us to lay down the parts of ourselves that are unholy or inconsistent with Him and burn them up completely on the divine altar of sacrifice.[6] Without which, our commitment may be too shallow[7] to continue in the faith and live even higher and holier laws, such as consecration.

As taught to the early school of the elders, "A religion that does not require the sacrifice of all things, never has power sufficient to produce the faith necessary unto life and salvation."[8] Deep sacrifice fosters deep commitment.[9] Sacrificing our natural will is a holy pattern, a divine order, and a necessary attribute to create lives fit for the kingdom to one day govern and reign in eternity as exalted beings. Thus, "Whoso layeth down his life in my cause, for my name's sake, shall find it again, even life eternal" (D&C 98:13). Or, "All among [you] who know their hearts are honest, and are broken, and their spirits contrite, and are willing to observe their covenants by sacrifice—yea, every sacrifice which I, the Lord, shall command—they are accepted of me" (D&C 97:8).

While we may be understandably fearful to sacrifice for God, and we must lean on our faith in Christ to overrule our fears, let us never despair of letting go by divine decree. Our sacrifices likely will cause discomfort, be challenging, or even bring pain (would it be a true sacrifice without it?), but the eventual reward will be greater than that which is released.[10]

THE LAW OF SACRIFICE

Prophetic and scriptural teachings promise to give back with much more than we have ever let go,[11] even "an hundredfold now in this time . . . and in the world to come eternal life" (Mark 10:30).

THE LAW OF THE GOSPEL

In the temple we covenant to live the Lord's gospel. The law of the gospel centers on following our Savior, taking His name upon us by covenant, and being born again to become more holy like Christ in our character.[1]

Although we talk about "the gospel" often in the Church, sometimes it becomes so broad as to almost encompass anything to do with the Church, as though food storage and home evening (while both beneficial) are part of "the gospel." However, in scripture Jesus is very clear about what defines His gospel, repeatedly summarized by five things: faith, repentance, baptism, reception of the Holy Ghost, and enduring to the end by continuing in that covenant (see 3 Nephi

THE LAW OF THE GOSPEL

27:13–20; D&C 33:10–12; 39:6). "Yea, this is my gospel" (3 Nephi 27:21).

To have *faith* in Christ means that we trust in His saving divinity.

To *repent* means that we align our lives to conform to His teachings.

To be *baptized* means we make an authorized covenant commitment with Him to take His name upon us and keep His commandments.

To *receive the Holy Ghost* means we receive the gift of the Spirit and strive to listen to, follow, and be influenced by God's invisible influence.

To *endure to the end* means we continue in this trusting, covenant-committed relationship with Christ, consistently rededicating ourselves to our Redeemer.

AN EXPLANATION: LIVING THE GOSPEL

Living the gospel means that we have entered a relationship with our Lord. A deep, covenant-committed, intimate one at that. One of the most frequent metaphors Jesus used to describe His relationship with His loyal followers is the most intimate one we can understand: marriage. "I am married unto you," He plainly said to the Israelites (Jeremiah 3:14). "Thy maker is thine husband," Isaiah wrote (Isaiah 54:5).

We became metaphorically married to the Messiah

when we entered the waters of baptism and made a covenant with Him—a ceremony that greatly parallels a wedding. As in any marriage, when we join ourselves with Jesus in the gospel covenant, we become an heir with Him and gain access to all His gifts, powers, abilities, and virtues. His goodness becomes our goodness. His purity our purity. His holiness our holiness. That is why "the gospel" is translated and called "the good news."[2] The good news is that if we are His covenant people, He will purify, justify, and sanctify us, bringing us to heaven with Him despite our mortal weakness. That, indeed, is very good news.

"Living the gospel" means that we make and continue in that covenant relationship with Christ. We trust Him, we align our life with Him, we are committed to Him, we try to become one with Him through receiving the Spirit, and we loyally remain with Him. Each Sunday the Lord offers us a chance to recommit to Him, witnessing unto the Father by a covenant and ordinance, that we are truly one with Him. In a sense, when we partake of the sacrament, we renew our spiritual wedding vows. God, in turn, promises us we will always have the Lord's Spirit to be with us (see D&C 20:77, 79), which Spirit brings purification and sanctification to our souls (see 2 Nephi 31:17; Moroni 6:4). This steady, repeated spiritual cycle of faith, repentance, covenant commitment, and receiving the Spirit slowly brings about divine changes in our character. Peter says that this continued process "purifie[s] your souls in obeying the truth through the Spirit," resulting in "being born again" (1 Peter 1:23).

AN APPLICATION: LIVING THE HIGHER LAW

As we become reborn through repeatedly exercising faith, repenting, recommitting by covenant, and receiving the Spirit of God, our hearts and character are changed and transformed to be more like Christ. We leave behind rebellious telestial ways of living, progress past good-but-not-great terrestrial ways of being, and move on to celestial patterns that are more saintly and holy.

In other words, as we live the covenant to obey the gospel, we become changed to live the higher, celestial teachings of Jesus Christ, as taught in the Sermon on the Mount. The Sermon on the Mount is the Lord's handbook for living the higher law of His gospel. It doesn't encompass everything but lays out a general value system, or a divine and holy pattern, for someone seeking to follow Jesus.[3]

The Sermon on the Mount is found in Matthew 5–7, and an expanded and more complete version[4] is in 3 Nephi 12–14. In the Sermon, Jesus seeks to lift His listeners to an elevated way of living. He touches on anger, forgiveness, immorality, honesty, resisting evil, loving our enemies, fasting, praying, and seeking first God's kingdom, among many other things. He repeatedly starts a teaching by saying, "It hath been said by them of old time . . ." and then repeats a former lower-level teaching, but then supplants it with a, "But I say unto you . . ." and gives a higher, holier way to live.

He says, in essence: This is how a telestial person would handle this, here's how a terrestrial person may, and here's how a celestial one should. For example, a telestial way is to commit adultery, and a terrestrial way would be to not commit adultery but still indulge in immoral thoughts and ideas, but Jesus says, "But I say unto you, that whosoever looketh on a woman, to lust after her, hath committed adultery already in his heart. Behold, I give unto you a commandment, that ye suffer none of these things to enter into your heart" (3 Nephi 12:28–29). He does the same thing with violence: Telestial people kill, terrestrial don't kill but still become enraged, but celestial people should not let anger linger, instead seeking to reconcile offenses with others (see 3 Nephi 12:21–25). Telestial people hate most anyone but themselves, terrestrial people love their friends but hate their enemies, celestial people love everyone, even those who "despitefully use you

THE LAW OF THE GOSPEL

and persecute you" (3 Nephi 12:44). The higher teachings of the Sermon are marvelous, and marvelously challenging. Through them our gospel character is being tested, not just our gospel knowledge.

A MOTIVATION: UNHOLY LAUGHTER AND TALK

As we strive for Christlike character, we also strive to leave behind everything that is unholy, vain, trifling, inappropriate, or rude. This doesn't mean that we don't have fun, laugh, and joke, or merely walk around solemn and sad-faced all the time. "A merry heart doeth good," after all (Proverbs 17:22). Clearly, we can and should have a healthy sense of humor[5] and cheerfully enjoy life.[6] But we should do it at the right time and in the right way, and if we are in sacred settings we act in a way consistent with those ideals. Joseph Smith wrote that "the things of God are of deep import, and time and experience, and careful and ponderous and solemn thoughts can only find them out."[7]

Thus, a crude, crass, or careless approach to spiritual things is inconsistent with endowment.[8] The Lord told some of the early elders in the School of the Prophets that to be endowed with power, you should "cast away your idle thoughts and your excess of laughter far from you" (D&C 88:69) and to "cease from all your light speeches . . . from all your pride and light-mindedness" (D&C 88:121). That's why in the temple we don't speak or laugh loudly.[9] Joseph Smith taught the early elders seeking endowment in the Kirtland Temple that they should be "solemn . . . without any talking or confusion . . . in silent prayer."[10] We can't be flippant and expect to be powerful. Sacredness and seriousness go together like pricelessness and carefulness. The higher teachings of holiness also include avoiding other impure behaviors such as laziness, fault-finding (see D&C 88:124), and evil speaking[11] of the Lord's anointed servants.[12]

While these high ideals stretch each of us, line upon line, and grace by grace, God can make them part of our character and being as we obey the gospel covenant. The Beatitudes at the beginning of the Sermon on the Mount are meant to illustrate this progressive growth.[13] They describe someone who is in a "blessed" state—someone who comes unto the Savior, enters the covenant, seeks to live His holy teachings, and becomes like Him in His divine character.[14] Living the law of the gospel is a process whereby we try to follow this blueprint, become born again, attain the holy attributes of the Son of God, and thus hear the words, "Blessed are ye . . ."

THE LAW OF CHASTITY

It used to confuse me why chastity was included as part of the endowment covenants. Why not obedience, sacrifice, the gospel, and the law of *service*? Why not covenant to live the law of *peace* ("blessed are the peacemakers," says Matthew 5:9) or something like the law to *preach the gospel* (see D&C 42:6)? Why is a specific behavior like chastity suddenly sandwiched in the middle of broader concepts like sacrifice and consecration? It seems self-evident, after all, that not fornicating or committing adultery is subsumed in the greater laws of obedience and the gospel. We don't specifically covenant not to murder or steal, so why covenant to not have sexual relations outside of marriage? There are likely a few good reasons, but a major one is this:

The law of chastity is not just about sex.

That's an admitted overstatement to grab attention, but it's helpful to help shift our thinking about this central human desire. The law of chastity is situated between greater principles because being chaste encompasses greater principles itself. The law of chastity is about trust; it is about righteous use of power; it is about care; it is about creation; it is about covenant family.

AN EXPLANATION: POWERFUL CHASTITY

Before I go on, a clear definition of the law of chastity is necessary. One used by the prophets is that living the law of chastity means to be "sexually pure before marriage and faithful within marriage,"[1] or "having no sexual activity except with those to whom they are legally and lawfully wedded according to God's law."[2] These are clear and useful definitions. More is needed, however, to explain some purposes to that law. So, here's a *why* definition about living the law of chastity: *The law of chastity means using your sexual capacities to earn trust, to respect agency, to righteously use power, to create children, and to strengthen marriage and family.*

To be clear, human sexuality is a good thing. We should not feel ashamed about our desires to be

THE LAW OF CHASTITY

physically intimate with someone else. They are *not* part of our "natural man" to get rid of, as discussed in the previous chapters. They are the very wellspring of life, divinely implanted[3] to create and maintain an eternal union and family. Prophets use words like "beautiful" and "sacred" and "ordained of God"[4] when describing marital sexual intimacy. President M. Russell Ballard said, "Be positive about how wonderful and beautiful physical intimacy can be when it happens within the bounds the Lord has set, including temple covenants and commitments of eternal marriage."[5] Elder David A. Bednar summarized marital sexual relations as "one of the ultimate expressions of our divine nature and potential."[6]

Although the innate human desire to create children, form families, and have intimate union with someone symbolized in sexual expression is heaven-sent, that divine desire becomes adulterated when it becomes unrestrained, prideful, domineering, manipulative, rude, or selfish. *Those* uses of the divine desire are the unwanted natural man and woman we do need to overcome. There is a reason why sex has been compared to fire:[7] sexual intimacy has the power to warm, to create, to purify, but it also has the power to burn, to destroy, and to engulf. Chaste people know how to care for the fire and use it properly without scorching themselves or another person, or—just as important—putting out the flame.

Remember, an overall purpose of the endowment is to help us learn to live like God, or to pattern our life after the order of the Son of God. And God is a being who uses power wisely, purposefully, and with temperance (or self-control). These characteristics allow God to create and maintain an eternal family, and to have us as His children completely trust Him, or in other words, have *faith*. True power is found in self-control.

AN APPLICATION: PLUMB, SQUARE, AND LEVEL

While some in our modern society of moral relativism and freedom of expression bristle when lines are drawn related to human sexuality, they forget that power without bounds is the foundation of both corruption and chaos. Remember, even God has boundaries in which He abides and won't cross, or He "would cease to be God" (Alma 42:22, 25). What a revolutionary doctrine! As we learn to properly control power and abide within covenant boundaries, we learn to become more like God.

One cannot have lasting faith in a person who is not morally aligned. Becoming a high priestly person endowed with God's power is a lot like building a wall.

THE LAW OF CHASTITY

When you frame a wall, you use established building standards. You measure off the studs and double nail them at sixteen-inch increments to a bottom and top board. You snap a chalk line on the ground to align the bottom board, so you know its straight. After you've lined up where the bottom of the wall should go, you level and plumb it vertically so it stands upright at ninety degrees. When it's properly measured, fastened, aligned, plumbed, and leveled, you've likely created a wall that can stand for hundreds of years.

Conversely, walls that aren't built this way don't last as long. They can't hold the weight of the building properly. They quickly begin to lean or tip because they don't meet established codes. Given time and pressure, they will collapse or need to be pulled down and properly reconstructed.

Thus, power and selfish interests must always be kept in check. There is a reason why the United States Constitution, which God inspired (see D&C 101:78–80), was set up with checks and balances through its various branches, so that no one person or group lets power go unrestrained to the national detriment. For sexual expression, there are always restraints, checks, and balances, before marriage and after.[8] At minimum, there are three related to sex:

THE HOLY COVENANTS

1. What God desires.
2. What you desire.

And a third when you become married:

3. What your spouse desires.

Like plumb, square, and level, those three must all be in harmony and brought together with trilateral consent. With sexual intimacy, we can't righteously say, "I want this" if our spouse does not. We can't say, "We want this" if God does not. And nobody should require, "God wants this" if either party does not, impelling contrary to agency. Alignment in all three areas is necessary. In a loving relationship there's no place for being disrespectful or domineering—the exact opposite virtues this eternal law is seeking to build within us. Instead, trust, kindness, tenderness, consideration,[9] and consent are the virtues that create not only true intimacy but long-lasting relationships.[10]

Whether we are single, dating, or married—young or old—framing the law of chastity in the broader context of earning trust, respecting agency, circumscribing passions, and righteously using power provides practical daily application to help us learn to be more moral. While not exhaustive, consider the following questions in each of these categories:

THE LAW OF CHASTITY

Trust: Am I straightforward and honest with others? Do I avoid conveniently lying or giving half-truths to my teachers, coworkers, friends, or family to get my way? Do I do what I say I will do? Am I where I should be when I should be there? Am I dependable? Can people confide in me?

Respect: Do I treat others as my equals? Do I avoid demeaning people who are a different age, gender, race, social class, religion, orientation, or education? Am I kind to strangers? Do I keep boundaries that others give me? Do I ask before I take something? Am I concerned with others' feelings? Am I careful with other people's property and valued things?

Circumscribing Passions: Do I seek to be temperate in my actions? Do I keep my spending within a budget? Do I control my temper at sporting events or while driving on the road? If healthy, do I fast for two meals or a twenty-four-hour period? Do I avoid saying some things I think? Do I walk away from a heated conversation? Do I proactively choose quality media?

Power: Do I make myself an exception to rules I expect others to follow? Do I pressure others or emotionally manipulate to get my way? Do I twist facts or information to come across as looking good? Do I cheat to win? Do I push others down to push myself up? Do I use threats, aggressiveness, or bullying to subdue others who stand in my way?

To be clear, none of these questions alone means we are or aren't chaste. I don't want to misconstrue the law to look beyond the mark. Rather, I mention these to help illustrate how consciously working to acquire these broader traits undergirds the greater principles of being "moral" and enables the virtues and power necessary to maintain eternal lives. "Let virtue garnish thy thoughts unceasingly; *then* shall thy confidence wax strong in the presence of God" (D&C 121:45; emphasis added). The endowment, with its emphasis on chastity and virtue, is preparing us for confidence in the presence of God.

A MOTIVATION: CREATING CHASTITY

With these broader celestial principles that support this law in mind, let us therefore understand that chastity is *created*. As one writer aptly summarized, "Chastity is not something you are born with and then break or lose, it is something that is made."[11] While not excusing its misuse, governing sexual desire can be unwieldy at times and will likely involve missteps. There will be flare-ups and letdowns, slips and falls, singes and burns. Thus, like riding a bike, early on we often need training wheels and guardians holding on

THE LAW OF CHASTITY

to the rear of our seats for a while. We may crash every now and then as we learn to ride on our own, sometimes painfully. But eventually, by learning how to balance and steer things right, freedom and possibilities become open to us. Let us be patient as we learn to understand how to handle sexual power, perhaps the most potent one we are given.[12]

In this vein of thought, it is important to also see that sex is not only about marriage. In mortality, some may be single, others divorced, and others in a marriage that lacks sexual intimacy for various reasons. While not undermining the centrality of the family and its role in living an exalted life, our goal in life is not just to have a family, but to become holy beings who can maintain eternal families. Remember, we make the covenant of chastity before any of us enter an eternal marriage. Those who are working to wisely handle passionate power through governing sexual desires are building the foundation for an eternal family, married or single.

That complete dedication to a spouse and to God—making covenants for current and future marriage—creates the oneness needed to endure in the eternities. At some point in our mortal probations, all of us must learn to be chaste if we are to ever reign on thrones as principled, selfless, dedicated, trustworthy, and wise users of God's power, as absolute integrity is required. That is what the covenant family is based upon. Alma told his son Shiblon to "bridle all your passions, that *ye may be filled with love*" (Alma 38:12; emphasis added). Controlling power, earning trust, circumscribing passions, and respecting others enables us to have eternal love, or as the scriptures say, to have "increase" or a "continuation of the seeds" (D&C 131:4; 132:19). Learning to live as a wise governor of procreative power in mortality is the litmus test for maintaining that wonderful power in eternity.

Chastity is a celestial law for a reason.

THE LAW OF CONSECRATION

The law of consecration is the pinnacle covenant of the endowment ceremony, and a key to living after the holy order of the Son of God. The irony is that for such a crucial covenant, it may also be among the most misunderstood.[1] I was once talking with a priesthood leader who told me about an anonymous man whom he had interviewed to renew his temple recommend. When the priesthood leader asked the man, "Do you keep the covenants that you made in the temple?" the man responded with, "Only the ones God has asked me to keep." Puzzled, the priesthood leader asked, "Which do you think He has not asked you to keep?" Could you imagine if the man had said "chastity" or "obedience"? Instead, he said, "The law of consecration." When pressed about why he didn't think he was asked to live that covenant, the man said something like, "Well, I'm not asked to give everything over to the bishop, so how can I?"

His answer reveals a crucial misunderstanding about the law of consecration, and he's not alone. I once did a pre-class quiz with over seven hundred BYU students in a Doctrine and Covenants class. One of the questions dealt with their understanding of consecration. Half the students selected the option that said consecration is only *partly* practiced in the Church through tithes and offerings, *but not in full*—as though tithing is somehow a "lesser," law-of-Moses interim and we're waiting for future full consecration. As further evidence of this, thirty-one percent said that consecration was not practiced at all in the Church today but will one day be brought back in the Millennium. Only seventeen percent of my BYU students said that consecration is "practiced in full in the Church today."

To be clear, the law of consecration is fully in force, and is kept and practiced by countless covenant-keeping Latter-day Saints today.[2] We are not, collectively, living a lower version of it, nor are we waiting for some prophetic announcement nor Jesus to usher in the Millennium to restart it. The law of consecration is "a covenant and a deed which cannot be

THE LAW OF CONSECRATION

broken" (D&C 42:30). It is a celestial law. It may be *the* celestial law.[3] Indeed, consecration is the very essence of complete dedication that defines those who will be exalted in the kingdom of God.[4]

AN EXPLANATION: DEDICATING OURSELVES

Much of the misunderstanding with consecration is definitional. Some think that because some Church members attempted to implement consecration in one way at one time, that is the only way it should be implemented for all time. Don't confuse laws, however, with applications of laws, or principles with practices. Practices like giving everything to the bishop (and him giving back property according to needs—a great system for poor Saints to pool resources in frontier Missouri) or united Church business firms in Kirtland or cooperative stores in Utah or tithing storehouses and welfare programs everywhere are all *applications* of the law, but they aren't the law itself.[5] Applications change, yet laws remain. To think that we don't live the law of consecration today because we don't meet with the bishop to hand over all our property is like thinking we don't live the law of sacrifice because we don't meet with a priest to hand over a lamb.

So that we have a clear definition on the broader law, I offer this one as a summary of prophetic teachings: The law of consecration is that as God's agent, you dedicate your time, talents, and means to building up God's kingdom on earth as He directs you.[6] To consecrate means to dedicate something or to set it apart as holy.[7] Just as we do with the laws of chastity or obedience, we first commit to dedicate (or consecrate) our lives to God at baptism. Faithful Latter-day Saints renew and deepen their covenant of consecration to God in the holy temple. The Church's booklet *Preparing to Enter the Holy Temple* says that through consecration, "We covenant to give of our resources in time and money and talent—all we are and all we possess—to the interest of the kingdom of God upon the earth."[8]

Consecration is not merely monetary and cannot be reduced to communal economics. Consecration involves our very beings—our breath, our bodies, our abilities, our opportunities.[9] Those who try to equate consecration to communism—Smith to Marx—so fundamentally misunderstand the law as to compare a lawnmower to a car simply because they both have wheels. Their central purposes and principles are so radically different as to make comparisons comical. Yes, consecration is partly communal, including caring for the poor and needy temporally (see D&C 42:30–31), but it is mostly celestial. It is a complete commitment to God. Living the law of consecration involves using our time in accordance with how God wants us to use it, using our talents and abilities to do and promote His will, and using our temporal gifts the way God desires, all done by Spirit-directed agency with the intent to build up the Lord's kingdom on the earth.[10]

Some struggle to see a difference between the law of sacrifice and the law of consecration. There are areas of overlap, of course, but they have some fundamental differences. Sacrifice is to give things up; consecration is to dedicate them to God, but often we retain them. Sacrifice is the release of the unholy; consecration retains to make holy. Where sacrifice is about letting go of our will, consecration is about absorbing God's will. Sacrifice, chastity, obedience, and the gospel each contribute and prepare us to fully implement the law of consecration.[11]

AN APPLICATION: CONSECRATION IN THE DOCTRINE AND COVENANTS

God first revealed ideas related to the law of consecration as early as 1831. The simplest summary comes in Doctrine and Covenants 42, the section known as the law of the Church: "Behold, thou wilt remember the poor, and consecrate of thy properties for their support that which thou hast to impart unto them"

(v. 30).¹² As the years progressed, other revelations and principles related to implementing the law of consecration were given (see D&C 52; 78; 82; 104; 119). Thus, the Doctrine and Covenants becomes one of the best scriptural guides to know how to understand and live the law of consecration. When we covenant to live the law of consecration, we are covenanting to accept it according to how it is taught in these revelations. Three consistent principles to live the law of consecration as taught in the Doctrine and Covenants are *ownership*, *stewardship*, and *agency/accountability*.¹³

Ownership: The principle of ownership means we understand that God owns everything. If we want to understand what we truly own, ask ourselves what we will take with us when we die. Everything we have on this earth is a gift. Doctrine and Covenants 104:14 states, "I, the Lord, stretched out the heavens, and built the earth, my very handiwork; and all things therein are mine." In fact, the Lord wants us to understand this point so much that He says "all things are mine" *four times* in that same consecration-laced section (see D&C 104:14–14, 55–56). The dust of the earth, the elements of its creation, all things upon the face thereof, even our very mortal bodies are not ours, but God's (see 1 Corinthians 6:19–20). Thus, if we are not owners, the next logical principle of consecration is that we are stewards.

Stewardship: The Lord said in Doctrine and Covenants 42:32: "Every [person] shall be . . . a steward over [his or her] own property." Stewardship implies being a temporary overseer of something. Yet it isn't ours. Even though I might say, "This is my home," it isn't really. I am just a steward over it—a temporary controller—paying the mortgage and momentarily holding a title to it. One day this home and the land it sits on will slip right out of my hands to someone else to become its steward. While it is in my care, however, I oversee it and try to do with it as pleases God. I retain the home, but I've dedicated it to God in prayer not just to protect it from a potential fire or flood, but more important, *for His purposes*. The same is true of our time and our talents. We momentarily have these bodies, these minds, these opportunities, these callings, these abilities, these temporalities. We seek to consecrate them in a way that pleases God as the giver. "God, what would you have me do with my_____?" we pray. "Father, I've decided to do _____ with my time; does that please you?" "Lord, I want to pursue _____ with my abilities; is that in harmony with your desires?" These kind of internal dialogues with Deity indicate the mind of a faithful, consecrated steward.

Agency and Accountability: As stewards, therefore, the third principle of consecration is that we are agents who are accountable to the owner. The Lord said, "It is expedient that I, the Lord, should make every [person] accountable, as a steward . . . and to be agents unto themselves" (D&C 104:13, 17). Because I am a steward, I will account to God with what I did with my abilities, my opportunities, my time, my life, my choices. I say "my," but I say that in the spirit of "His"—a steward who has merely been privileged to act with these things as an agent. "Agency" doesn't only mean the ability to choose; it also means the power to represent and proactively act on behalf of someone.[14] As consecrated stewards, we are the Lord's agents to bring about His business. One of the great things about consecrated agency is that the Lord doesn't need to tell us everything to do. We know His general will, and He doesn't need to always give specific "go and do" directives. God says, "It is not meet that I should command in all things. . . . Verily I say, men should be anxiously engaged in a good cause, and do many things of their own free will, and bring to pass much righteousness, for the power is in them, wherein they are agents unto themselves" (D&C 58:26–27). Some of our best consecration is when we use our agency and choose to dedicate our time, talents, and means for good, even if God doesn't command or directly tell us to do it. We are proactively learning to live like God as that happens.

A MOTIVATION: LIVING CONSECRATION TODAY

We need not wait for any new divine directive to live this eternal law of consecration today. We can implement the principles of ownership, stewardship, and agency/accountability in our lives right now. Three things that can help us fully live the law of consecration today are:

1. Implement current general prophetic directives regarding time, talents, and means. Pay tithing, pay a generous fast offering, serve in Church callings, minister to assigned members. Those are basics for us all.
2. Ask God in prayer how He would have us individually use our time, talents, and means, and then follow personal promptings from the Holy Ghost. We each have a unique life's mission. Ask God what He would have you do with what He's given you personally, and then follow it to fulfill your mortal purposes to build His kingdom.
3. As an agent who represents God, proactively use our agency to serve others with our

time, talents, and means. Choose to bring about God's will and help people overcome the effects of the Fall. For example: help educate, ease someone's pain, eliminate injustice, balance unfairness, feed the hungry, befriend someone who is lonely. All of these contribute to establishing God's kingdom on this earth and helping God's will be done perfectly on earth as it is in heaven.

Utilize daily prayer as touch points for consecration. In the morning, dedicate your day to God to strive to do His will and follow His directives, using your time, talents, and means in ways that would please Him. At night, return and report what you've done and pay special attention to any celestial response from the Spirit further directing you.[15] Thus, as one example, if God prompts you to attend college and you do, that's consecration! You are spending your time in class, enhancing and using your talents in learning, and utilizing your means to pay for tuition, books, and fees, all to help do and bring about God's will as He directs you. Similarly, if you get a few extra dollars from work and you feel to give it to someone in need, that's also consecration. If you willingly drive the ward youth to youth conference, that's consecration.

THE LAW OF CONSECRATION

If you proactively choose to help a neighbor in need with yard work, that's consecration. Each of these is an example of covenant Saints dedicating their time, talents, and means to building up God's kingdom on earth as He directs them in their individual stewardship and agency.

My wife, thinking of consecration, once said to me, "Everyone has needs and everyone has abundance." We should ask ourselves where we've been given an abundance and how we can offer it to the Lord, His Church, or His children.[16] Maybe you've been blessed with abundant optimism, or you're at a period of life where you have extra discretionary time, or you're naturally good at math. There's likely someone within reach who is low on hope, needs an evening visit, or is struggling with statistics (there are lots of those!). And equally, we're each in need of something ourselves and can likely benefit from the kind offering of others. When God has thousands of servants who have consecrated their all to Him, He can build His kingdom on earth. Consecrated women and men will be the ones prepared to inherit that kingdom as dedicated queens and kings, receiving a fulness of God's promised blessings.

PART III
THE POWER

"Those holding the fulness of the [Melchizedek] priesthood are kings and Priests to the most high God, holding the keys of power and blessings."
—JOSEPH SMITH

THE ENDOWMENT OF POWER

Although we may be on our way because of the temple covenants we have received, we have not yet arrived to a "fulness" of the priesthood and glory of God, as the scriptures describe it (see D&C 93:19–20; D&C 124:28). No, not even close. That will take a lifetime (or more) of learning and experience. But we have received promised blessings from God for those who enter and continue on the covenant path after the holy order of His Son. Some of those promised blessings are available to us here and now in mortality, and some of them await their fulfillment in eternity. Three specific promised blessings are:

1. Power to be endowed with spiritual gifts.
2. Power to become the elect of God.
3. Power to become exalted.

POWER TO BE ENDOWED WITH SPIRITUAL GIFTS

Doctrine and Covenants 107:18–19 gives perhaps the best summary of mortal blessings for receiving the ordinances and living the covenants of the temple:

> The power and authority of the higher, or Melchizedek Priesthood, is to hold the keys of all the spiritual blessings of the church—To have the privilege of receiving the mysteries of the kingdom of heaven, to have the heavens opened unto them, to commune with the general assembly and church of the Firstborn, and to enjoy the communion and presence of God the Father, and Jesus the mediator of the new covenant.

In other words, through temple ordinances and covenants, in this life we are promised spiritual power; power to receive revelation ("the mysteries of the kingdom of heaven"); power to call upon the heavens and have them hear us ("to have the heavens opened unto them"); power to have the promised ministering of angels to help us ("to commune with the general assembly and church of the Firstborn"); power to truly come to know our Savior, Jesus Christ, and God our Father and to have a personal relationship with them ("enjoy the communion and presence of God the Father, and Jesus the mediator of the new covenant").

Through the endowment we are promised power in this life to perform marvelous works and miracles beyond our own abilities;[1] power to discern truth from error;[2] power to more deeply understand God's purposes and plans for His children, individually and collectively; power to have increased hope and peace in the midst of the daily demands and difficulties of life.[3]

This is the mortal *endowment of power* that was promised by God ever since 1831 (see D&C 38:32). Maybe we've experienced some of these spiritual powers in our life already, and maybe we yet will in future years. They are real, however, and they are really needed. We may be tempted to think that this kind of power applies only to those who lead the Church (like the First Presidency and the Twelve) because of their callings, but they can also happen for everyday Saints because of their covenants. Remember, ordinances activate the powers of godliness in our lives (see D&C 84:20–21). Do not doubt and fear like some members of the early School of the Prophets did, otherwise we won't receive and experience this endowment of spiritual power (see D&C 67:3). Whatever we do, let's not sell ourselves short and live beneath our spiritual privileges.[4] Let us not lose spiritual horizons[5] as we shuffle with our heads down through mortality. Let us lift up our eyes and see the vistas of spiritual endowment that can be ours as we live our covenants (see John 4:35).

POWER TO BECOME THE ELECT OF GOD

With so many in the world who are confused about their identity and purpose, as we enter into and follow the holy covenant order of God, we will see more clearly the true purposes of mortality. As we comprehend this exalted vision, we will taste the love of God and be filled with the great gift of charity. As we experience the love of God, we will naturally want to share that love with others. The temple will not absolve us from the challenges of mortality, but it will give us the knowledge, strength, vision, and ability to overcome them through the grace of God. His name is and will be upon us, arming us with power, glory, and angels to have charge over us and help us in our daily lives (see D&C 109:22).

This power becomes ours through priesthood covenants and how, by virtue of them, we can become the elect, or chosen children of God (see Mosiah 27:25;

Ether 3:14; D&C 25:1). One section of the Doctrine and Covenants that deals with this in a temple-centric theme is section 84. In this section we learn that God intends to build a holy temple so His glory can be there (see vv. 4–5). He teaches that the "sons of Moses and of Aaron" who enter that temple (this is all of God's Church and people, women and men, who serve in the temple; see D&C 128:24) will be "filled with the glory of the Lord . . . in the Lord's house" (D&C 84:32). The Lord promises that if we will be "faithful unto the obtaining these two priesthoods," or the covenant promises of the Aaronic and Melchizedek priesthood available to both men and women,[6] we become "the seed of Abraham" and part of the "church and kingdom" and specifically "the elect of God" (v. 34). This is because if we receive these priesthood covenants, we receive Jesus and have His name upon us. And if we receive Jesus, we will receive God our Father, and therefore we are promised His "Father's kingdom" and "all that [His] Father hath" (vv. 35–38). That is God's oath and covenant, which "he cannot break," that belongs to the ordinances of the priesthood found in the holy temple (see vv. 39–40).

POWER TO BECOME EXALTED

Thus, if we will live faithful to the holy covenant

patterns taught to us in the temple, one day we will receive the fulness of God's priesthood, or all that He has. We will receive "thrones, kingdoms, principalities, and powers, dominions" (D&C 132:19). Those thus exalted in the celestial kingdom will be "priests and kings [and priestesses and queens], who have received of his fulness . . . after the order of Melchizedek" (D&C 76:56–57).

Importantly, this promise of exaltation is familial. There are no solo monarchs in heaven—no king without a queen, or vice versa. While salvation is individual, exaltation is matrimonial.[7] One of the crowning doctrinal ideas of the Restoration is that women and men can become like God, but to do so they must "enter into this order of the priesthood [meaning the new and everlasting covenant of marriage]" (D&C 131:2).

While there are numerous factors that influence whether someone can have an eternal marriage in this life (many out of one's own control), prophets have repeatedly taught that all who make and keep their covenants with God will have the promise of eternal life and exaltation afforded to them, including the blessings of eternal marriage and family.[8] The purpose of mortality is not to form perfect families. None of us will have or experience that, as all families are fallen to some degree. The purpose of life is to know and become like Christ so one day we can form eternal families. The covenants we make in the endowment ceremony not only prepare us to one day become like our Heavenly Parents, but they prepare us to live in an eternal marriage covenant like they do. We cannot create eternal families without being humble, obedient, chaste, sacrificing, or being dedicated—first to God but also to each other. As the covenant of baptism prepares and points to the endowment, the endowment covenants prepare and point to an eternal marriage.[9] And the eternal marriage covenant prepares and points us to progress toward exaltation.

With an eternal marriage, a couple can "pass by the angels, and the gods, which are set there, to their exaltation and glory in all things, as hath been sealed upon their heads, which glory shall be a fulness and a continuation of the seeds forever and ever. Then shall they be gods" (D&C 132:19–20). These eternal blessings are *promissory*, secured upon us if we honor and keep our temple covenants.[10] They have not yet taken effect, nor will they until they are "sealed unto [us] by the Holy Spirit of promise, by him who is anointed" (D&C 132:19).

This, really, is what the Restoration is all about. It isn't just about restoring "the Church," but about restoring the covenant family of God. It is about restoring our mortal relationships, our earthly ties to spouses, children, parents, siblings, and loved ones that are bound by celestial priesthood powers. It is about restoring us to our intended condition of fulfilled divine potential, on a perfected celestial earth, where gods and goddesses are enthroned with eternal power, glory, dominion, and increase. The temple ordinances and covenants—hinting constantly through progressive rooms and priesthood orders—not only promise these blessings but help us momentarily see and taste them as we participate in the endowment ceremony. Through it, we can catch a glimpse of our eternal identity and purpose.

THE TASTE OF ETERNITY

Although my given name is Anthony, growing up everyone knew me as Tony. I was called "T-bone" by one family member and "Big T" by another, along with "Tony Bologna" and "Tony Macaroni"!

When I left for a mission, I was suddenly called Elder Sweat. For two years, most didn't even know my first name. "Elder Es-weat!" they would call me in beautiful Bolivian accents.

I came home and shortly thereafter got married. My wife decided to change her last name. We were now the "Sweats," plural (admittedly, that sounds funny).

A few years later we had our first child. The first name she ever called me was "Dadda" (admittedly, that sounds awesome).

THE HOLY COVENANTS

I got hired to teach seminary for the Church Educational System. On a black placard mounted to a gray carpeted wall was my newest name, "Brother Sweat."

In grad school, I decided to stop correcting professors when they called me by my official printed name. "Anthony, what do you think?" they would inquire. Anthony started responding.

When I published my first book, I did it under my given name. Soon, people were writing emails or talking about me as "Anthony Sweat," the author. Although close friends and family still call me Tony, even today, "Anthony Sweat" is how I'm known by most professionally and publicly.

At the time I launched my Instagram account, I combined some of my public names into the handle @brotheranthonysweat

I then got hired to be a university professor. "Professor Sweat" and "Dr. Sweat" got added to the list of names by which I'm known and called by many.

I recently received another when I was called to a new calling that carries a congregational title: "Bishop Sweat."

With this list, I often get people asking me what they should call me or how they should introduce me. Am I Tony, Anthony, Brother Sweat, Anthony Sweat, Dr. Sweat, Professor Sweat, Bishop Sweat? The truth is my name is all of those, but at the same time, it's none of them.

So, who am I?

Amidst an agitated crowd at the temple, some people had a similar question for Jesus. "Who art thou?" they demanded. Are you Jesus of Nazareth? Jesus the craftsman, the son of Mary and Joseph? Should we call you Yeshua, or "Joshua," your Aramaic name? Are you a rabbi, a teacher? Are you like Elias, or Jeremiah, a prophet? Are you the Messiah, the anointed one to save, the Christ? Just who exactly are you?

"I am the light of the world," He answers.

They wonder, what kind of identifier is that? What are you saying?

"Why do ye not understand my speech?" Jesus asks, responding for them Himself. "Even because ye cannot hear my word."

"Thou art a Samaritan," someone retorts, condescendingly.

Not just a Samaritan, but perhaps illegitimate. "Born of fornication," is jabbed out, maybe a slight at His mother.

"Thou hast a devil," someone shouts at Him.

THE HOLY COVENANTS

Just who on earth do you think you are? "Whom makest thou thyself?"

The accusing question hangs, lingering in air thick with tension.

Jesus, Joshua, the carpenter, the Nazarene, the rabbi, the teacher, the prophet. Who on earth are you?

And that's the problem. It is not an earthly identifier; it's a heavenly one.

Jesus breaks the silence, knowing exactly who He is.

"I am [Jehovah],[1]" He says audaciously, walking away from the bewildered and frenzied crowd (see John 8:12–59).

―――

How do we identify ourselves? Name ourselves? Label ourselves? The way we do so changes how we see ourselves. I've always been somewhat puzzled by God's presentation to Moses. Moses, understandably, was likely going through a bit of an identity crisis himself. Raised in Pharaoh's court, was he a Hebrew, a Levite, Pharaoh's grandson? Pharaoh's daughter named him "Moses," the water boy.[2] Was he a "prince" of Egypt? Jethro's son-in-law, the priest of Midian? A shepherd?

When God appeared and called him, even Moses asked, "God, who am I?" (Exodus 3:11).

Before answering, God first wants Moses to know who God is.

"Behold, I am the Lord God Almighty," "Endless is my name," "I am without beginning of days or end of years" (Moses 1:3). Then, the Lord shifts to addressing Moses's identity: "Behold, thou art my son," "I have a work for thee, Moses, my son," "Thou art in the similitude of mine Only Begotten," "This one thing I show unto thee, Moses, my son" (Moses 1:4–7). God shows Moses the works of His hands, the Creation, and the inhabitants of the earth, so much so that Moses marvels.

Well known in the story, Satan comes to tempt Moses, which Moses flatly rejects because Moses's vision and personal identity has been eternally elevated. "And it came to pass that Moses looked upon Satan and said: Who art thou? For behold, I am a son of God, in the similitude of his Only Begotten" (Moses 1:13). The tempter leaves with a temper tantrum. God returns. Visions open again. Identity is expanded. "I, the Almighty, have chosen thee," and God enlarges on Moses's earthly water name: "Thou shalt be made stronger than many waters; for they shall obey thy command as if thou wert God" (Moses 1:25). As if he were God! More visions flow. Truth floods over him. Awe overtakes him. Work and glory come to pass.

Moses, do you see this? Do you see them? Do you see yourself? Do you see who you really are, "my son"?

―⁓―

I received my patriarchal blessing when I was getting ready to head to college and at a crossroads. I was always a good-hearted kid. I cared about other people, although I was super competitive and had a temper that could compromise that disposition. At times, admittedly, I was more concerned with being cool than being kind. I went to seminary each day, church each week, and home teaching with my dad each month. But I cared more about being an all-state basketball player than being an all-stake priesthood servant. I had a serious girlfriend, with the serious issues those early relationships bring, and was way too serious about playing college sports. There was a pull, however, to serve a mission. I needed divine direction before I left home. I needed to figure out who I was.

I remember going to the patriarch's small, one-level house, all by myself. The room was shadowed by his east-facing home, orange '70s curtains letting some colored light spill through and bathe everything in an amber hue. A clock ticked quietly in the background. My six-foot-three frame felt the low ceilings too close. I sat on the couch, patiently, sensing importance even in my inexperience. The patriarch didn't talk to me much before he blessed me. I had never met him before. He pulled over a hard, brown chair from the kitchen and asked me to sit in it. He laid his old, wrinkled hands on my head, and spoke my name. "Anthony Ross Sweat . . ." he said in a commanding voice, and then he began to speak things about Anthony Ross Sweat that I had never conceived. I felt power. It flowed from his mouth through his hands into my mind and lodged in my heart, returning out my eyes. I tried to hold them back, but tears came. I let them spill, unaccustomed to such spiritual outpourings, wiping them hard with the back of my hand.

The patriarch spoke of Abraham, Isaac, Jacob, premortal valiance and associations, mortal missions and work, and eternal promises and potentials. It was as if, for a moment, the veil lifted for this random teenage boy, and I caught a glimpse of who I really was. I wasn't Anthony Sweat, Tony, or T-bone. I wasn't even the future professor, painter, or author. I was without beginning or end, a spirit child of God with a long premortal history and existence, a mortal who is here with covenant purpose and commitment, and one who has a future eternal identity, destiny, and exaltation if I am true to those covenants. The blessing closed, and heaven with it. I shook his hand, grabbed the brass doorknob, and got into my car. Mortality took forefront again as I signaled right and drove back to my middle-class, west-side, Utah home. But for a moment, I had tasted eternity.

⸻

Sometimes in the press of temporalities and telestial concerns, we become nearsighted. We see a day at a time, with its cares and calls, and it's about all we can manage. To-do lists and deadlines overwhelm us. Bills bury us. Emails and texts ping us. Failures beset us. We try to drown them out. We turn up the beats. We binge the latest show on Netflix. We escape in sports. We recreate. We shop. We scroll and double tap. We eat. We try to fill the hole. The world, and others caught in its ways, try to define us by our clothes, our possessions, where we live, the size of our home, our titles, our accomplishments, our followers, our appearance. One day, however, the thief of mortality will steal all of that away, moths and rust will corrupt it completely, and we will see that it is all vanity. So, who are we, really? What is our purpose? What is our true identity?

When we approach the temple and enter that royal heavenly palace, we feel as though we cross a liminal threshold. We pass through the doors and the world closes behind. We take off our dress shoes, silence cell phones, and change into simple white clothing. We hold packets of neatly folded priestly robes that remind us of our real identity and potential. Folded in shirt pockets or pinned to dress sleeves we carry mortal names of people who have lived and died before us, knowing those names—as special as they are—aren't really their true identity either. They lived before, and they continue to live on now. What were they or will they be called in heaven?

We wash and anoint, catching a glimpse of our divine identity and eternal potential. We are authorized to wear the garment to remind.[3] We go into the endowment rooms. We sense eternity. Like Moses, we learn of the great plan of God—the Creation, the Fall, the Atonement of Jesus Christ. Visions flow. Truth floods. Awe overtakes. Work and glory come to pass. We make covenants, we spiritually progress, we learn holy patterns of living, we go from telestial, to terrestrial, to celestial. We learn sacred, symbolic knowledge that represents this progress.[4] We are reminded that we are more than our mortal ages or accomplishments, careers or credentials, families or finances. We are to become priestesses and priests, queens and kings. We are to become modern Moseses and Melchizedeks, Sarahs and Rebekahs, Eves and Adams. And, with our vision expanded by ancient orders and eternal destinies, we learn about sacred names and potentials.

"And a white stone is given to each of those who come into the celestial kingdom, whereon is a new name written, which no man knoweth save he that receiveth it. The new name is the key word" (D&C 130:11). To "him that overcometh will I make a pillar in the temple of my God, and he shall go no more out: and I will write upon him the name of my God, and the name of the city of my God, which is new Jerusalem, which cometh down out of heaven from my God: and I will write upon him my new name" (Revelation 3:12).

In the endowment, we learn more deeply about God and Jesus, and therefore about ourselves (see John 7:17). In Joseph Smith's last great discourse of his life, he taught:

> Here then is eternal life, to know the only wise and true God. You have got to learn how to be Gods yourselves; to be kings and priests to God, the same as all Gods have done; by going from a small degree to another, from grace to grace, from exaltation to exaltation, until you are able to sit in glory as doth those who sit enthroned in everlasting power. . . . When you climb a ladder, you must begin at the bottom and

go on until you learn the last principle; it will be a great while before you have learned the last. It is not all to be comprehended in this world; it is a great thing to learn salvation beyond the grave. . . . When we know how to come to [God], he begins to unfold the heavens to us and tell us all about it. . . . I tell you these words of eternal life, that are given to me, I know you taste it.[5]

The temple helps us taste it. It helps us remember. It helps us see. President Russell M. Nelson taught that in the temple, "We learn of our eternal identity and purpose and the marvelous promises of the Lord."[6] The endowment helps us see beyond ourselves also, and fulfills the deep yearning to link our past, present, and future family[7]—connecting "roots and branches"[8]—the generations that came before and the ones that will come after. We see ourselves in the great chain of God's children, forged by the power of the holy priesthood and its ordinances, welded with past dispensations, sealed up to God and others (see D&C 128:18). It's a beautiful vision.

So, who am I? Who are you? Well, go to the temple, enter the order, taste eternal life, be anointed, touch the garment, put on the priestly clothes, catch

THE HOLY COVENANTS

the vision, make the covenants, live the patterns, learn the mysteries, progress, part the veils—both metaphorical and literal—and come into the presence of God. Listen to and think deeply about names, past, present, and future. See yourself in those names. Let those names become written onto you. Come to the modern-day school of the prophets and prophetesses. Learn how to tap into the powers of heaven, to be endowed with the powers of godliness through the temple ordinances and covenants. Then, you will be able to answer that question for yourself.

John Taylor asks us all:

> Have you forgot who you are, and what your object is? Have you forgot that you profess to be Saints of the Most High God, clothed upon with the Holy Priesthood? Have you forgot that you are aiming to become Kings and Priests to the Lord, and Queens and Priestesses to Him? Have you forgot that . . . you can learn the ways of life and salvation; where you are placed in a position that you can obtain blessings from the great Eloheim, that will rest upon you and your posterity worlds without end? Have you forgot these things?[9]

Let us not forget. Let us enter the temple, live the holy covenants, and taste eternity.

NOTES

Author's Note

1. Howard W. Hunter said we need to teach "more earnestly and more comfortably the things we can appropriately say about the purposes of the house of the Lord" (*Teachings of Presidents of the Church: Howard W. Hunter* [Salt Lake City: Intellectual Reserve, 2015], 184).

Part I: The Order

"Old Testament Revision 2," 39, The Joseph Smith Papers, https://www.josephsmithpapers.org/paper-summary/old-testament-revision-2/46; spelling modernized; see also Joseph Smith Translation, Genesis 14:26–27.

The Order of the Son of God

1. See Richard Neitzel Holzapfel, "The Nauvoo Temple," in *Joseph Smith, the Prophet and Seer*, 2010, 421–36. See also Devery Anderson, "The Anointed Quorum," *Journal of Mormon History*, vol. 29, no. 2, 2003, 137–57.
2. President Boyd K. Packer summarized the temple ceremonies similarly: "There, in a sacred ceremony, an individual may be washed and anointed and instructed and endowed and sealed" ("The Holy Temple," *Ensign*, Feb. 1995).
3. The full quote from Joseph Smith when he instituted the first endowment ceremony includes that he spent the day "instructing

NOTES

[participants] in the principles and order of the Priesthood, attending to washings, anointings, endowments and the communication of Keys pertaining to the Aaronic Priesthood, and so on to the highest order of Melchisedec Priesthood, setting forth the order pertaining to the ancient of Days, and all those plans and principles, by which any one is enabled to secure the fulness of those blessings, which have been prepared for the Church of the first born, and come up and abide in the presence of the Eloheim in the Eternal worlds. In this Council was instituted the Ancient order of things for the first time in these last days" ("History, 1838–1856, volume C-1 [2 November 1838–31 July 1842]," 1328, The Joseph Smith Papers, https://www.josephsmithpapers.org/paper-summary/history-1838-1856-volume-c-1-2-november-1838-31-july-1842/502).

4. See "Temples," *True to the Faith* (2004), 170–74.
5. "Natural capacity, power, or ability," http://www.merriam-webster.com/dictionary/endowment, or "A natural gift, ability, or quality," http://www.thefreedictionary.com/endowment.
6. The Lord directed the Saints in January 1831: "Ye should go to the Ohio . . . and there you shall be endowed with power from on high" (D&C 38:32). Church elders assembled at the Isaac Morley farm in June 1831 for a conference for the express purpose, in the words of attendee John Corrill, "that they might receive an endowment" (*John Corrill, Brief History*, as cited in *The Joseph Smith Papers, Documents, Volume 1, July 1828–June 1831* [2013], 318).
7. Joseph's history says at the June 1831 conference, "the authority of the melechisedec <priesthood> was manifested and <I> conferred, <the high priesthood> for the first time, upon several of the elders" ("History, 1838–1856, volume A-1 [23 December 1805–30 August 1834]," 118, The Joseph Smith Papers, https://www.josephsmithpapers.org/paper-summary/history-1838-1856-volume-a-1-23-december-1805-30-august-1834/124).
8. Editors for *The Joseph Smith Papers* write, "Jared Carter, for instance, associated the ability to perform miraculous healings with those ordained to the high priesthood" (Carter, Journal, 16–17). ("Historical Introduction for the "Minutes, circa 3–4 June 1831," 4, The Joseph Smith Papers, https://www.josephsmithpapers.org/paper-summary/minutes-circa-3-4-june-1831/2).
9. Speaking to some newly called high priests in Doctrine and Covenants 68, the Lord says, "You shall be given power to seal them up unto

NOTES

eternal life. Amen" (D&C 68:12). In October of 1831, the Prophet Joseph Smith taught that "the order of the High priesthood is that they have power given them to seal up the Saints unto eternal life" (Minute Book 2, 25–26 Oct. 1831, https://josephsmithpapers.org/paperSummary/minutes-circa-3-4-june-1831).

10. Ezra Booth, who was present at the June 1831 conference, later explained (after he left the Church) that those who had been "ordained to the High Priesthood, or the order of Milchesidec . . . profess to be endowed with the same power as the ancient apostles were" (Ezra Booth, "Mormonism—No. II," *Ohio Star* [Ravenna], 20 Oct. 1831, [3]).

11. "John Corrill, A Brief History of the Church of Christ of Latter Day Saints, 1839," 18, The Joseph Smith Papers, https://www.josephsmithpapers.org/paper-summary/john-corrill-a-brief-history-of-the-church-of-christ-of-latter-day-saints-1839/16.

12. See "History, 1838–1856, volume C-1 [2 November 1838–31 July 1842]," 1328, The Joseph Smith Papers, https://www.josephsmithpapers.org/paper-summary/history-1838-1856-volume-c-1-2-november-1838-31-july-1842/502.

13. "Nauvoo Relief Society Minute Book," 22, The Joseph Smith Papers, https://www.josephsmithpapers.org/paper-summary/nauvoo-relief-society-minute-book/19.

14. See Phoebe Woodruff, as cited in *The First Fifty Years of Relief Society: Key Documents in Latter-day Saint Women's History* (Salt Lake City: Church Historian's Press, 2016), 5.

15. See Doctrine and Covenants 107:3; 76:57; 124:23; Alma 13:1, 7, 16; Psalm 110:4; Hebrews 5:6.

16. See https://www.thesaurus.com/browse/order.

17. Ezra Taft Benson, "What I Hope You Will Teach Your Children about the Temple," *Ensign*, Aug. 1985.

18. See Russell M. Nelson, "A Plea to My Sisters," *Ensign*, Nov. 2015; see also "Spiritual Treasures" (*Ensign*, Nov. 2019). For a discussion on women and priesthood, including differences in terminology such as *offices* and *keys* from *power* and *authority*, see Dallin H. Oaks, "The Keys and Authority of the Priesthood" (*Ensign*, May 2014). For differences in the ecclesiastical Church and family or covenant priesthood, see Barbara Morgan Gardner, "Connecting Daughters of God with His Priesthood Power," *Ensign*, Mar. 2019; see also her book *The Priesthood Power of Women: In the Temple, Church, and Family* (Salt Lake City: Deseret Book, 2019).

NOTES

19. "Adam and his posterity were commanded by God to be baptized, to receive the Holy Ghost, and to enter into the order of the Son of God" (*Ensign*, Aug. 1985).
20. By living this order, I mean the order of high priests and priestesses, sealed into the order of eternal marriage. See Abraham 1:2–3; 2:2. The "blessings of the fathers" that Abraham refers to here include "making temple covenants and forming eternal families," according to former Relief Society General President Julie B. Beck ("Unlocking the Door to the Blessings of Abraham," BYU Devotional, March 2, 2008). Joseph Smith was endowed in May 1842 and Emma Smith endowed in September 1843 (see Devery Anderson, "The Anointed Quorum," *Journal of Mormon History*, vol. 29, no. 2, 2003, 137, 145).
21. References to the "holy order" in Alma include Alma 4:20; 5:54; 6:1; 7:22; 8:4, 43:2; 49:30; and eleven verses in Alma 13. A rival "order," after Amlici, later called the order of Nehors, is referenced in Alma 2:1; 14:16, 18; 15:15; 16:11; 21:4; and 24:28–30. See also Robert L. Millet, "The Holy Order of God," in *The Book of Mormon: Alma, the Testimony of the Word*, ed. Monte S. Nyman and Charles D. Tate Jr. (Provo, UT: Religious Studies Center, Brigham Young University, 1992), 61–88; Matthew S. Stenson, "Answering for His Order: Alma's Clash with the Nehors," *BYU Studies Quarterly* 55, no. 2 (2016): 127–53.
22. Brigham Young taught, "We have commenced to organize, I will say partially, in the Holy Order that God has established for his people in all ages of the world when he has had a kingdom upon the earth. We may call it the Order of Enoch, the Order of Joseph, the Order of Peter, or Abraham, or Moses" ("The Calling of the Priesthood, etc." *Journal of Discourses*, June 26, 1874, vol. 17, no. 17).
23. These major covenants have been repeatedly summarized in public by Church leaders and are summarized in the *General Handbook* (see section 27.2) as referenced and discussed in "The Why of Covenants" in this book.
24. Gordon B. Hinckley said that "temple blessings include our washings and anointings that we may be clean before the Lord" (First Presidency Message, "Temples and Temple Work," *Ensign*, Feb. 1982).
25. "The initiatory ordinances include special blessings regarding your divine heritage and potential. As part of these ordinances, you will also be authorized to wear the sacred temple garment" ("About the

NOTES

Temple Endowment," https://www.churchofjesuschrist.org/temples/what-is-temple-endowment?lang=eng).

26. "The endowment [teaches] participants to symbolically reenact key aspects of the plan of salvation" ("Temple Endowment," Church History Topics, https://www.churchofjesuschrist.org/study/history/topics/temple-endowment?lang=eng).

27. "You receive the remainder of your endowment in a group setting along with others who are attending the temple" where "the plan of salvation is presented, including the Creation of the world, the Fall of Adam and Eve, the Atonement of Jesus Christ, the Apostasy, and the Restoration" ("About the Temple Endowment," https://www.churchofjesuschrist.org/temples/what-is-temple-endowment?lang=eng). James E. Talmage wrote that the presentation of the endowment summarizes the plan of salvation, including "the most prominent events of the creative period, the condition of our first parents in the Garden of Eden, their disobedience and consequent expulsion from that blissful abode, their condition in the lone and dreary world when doomed to live by labor and sweat, the plan of redemption by which the great transgression may be atoned" (James E. Talmage, *House of the Lord: A Study of Holy Sanctuaries Ancient and Modern* [Salt Lake City: The Church of Jesus Christ of Latter-day Saints, 1912], 99–100).

28. "In ordinance rooms an overview is given of God's plan for His children. Latter-day Saints learn of their premortal and mortal lives, the creation of the world and the Fall of man, the central role of Jesus Christ as the Redeemer of all God's children, and the blessings they can receive in the next life. . . . The celestial room symbolizes the exalted and peaceful state that all may achieve through living the gospel of Jesus Christ. This room represents the contentment, inner harmony, and peace available to eternal families in the presence of Heavenly Father and His Son, Jesus Christ" ("Things Pertaining to This House," *Ensign*, Oct. 2010).

29. The term "mysteries of the kingdom of heaven" (D&C 107:19) is sometimes directly connected to the *ordinances* of the Melchizedek Priesthood, as in D&C 84:19–21. The term "mystery" is often thought of as something only known by revelation from God (see "Mysteries of God" in the *Guide to the Scriptures*). However, the word *mystery* comes from the Greek word *musterion/mysterion* (Strong's #3466), often used by Paul in his epistles, which some New Testament scholars connect to a religious drama that encapsulates a sacred secret—the

NOTES

greatest drama being enacted in Christ's suffering and death in the plan of salvation. *Musterion* is translated into the Latin Vulgate in some places as *sacramentum*, from which the English word "sacrament" derives. Thus, one way to look at the "mysteries of God" can be as a sacramental religious drama to reveal sacred, intimate knowledge of God. See Theodore B. Foster, "'Mysterium' and 'Sacramentum' in the Vulgate and Old Latin Versions" (*The American Journal of Theology*, Vol. 19, No. 3 (July 1915), 402–15); Emma Maggie Solberg, "A History of 'The Mysteries'" (*Early Theatre*, Vol. 19, No. 1 (2016), 9–36); see also https://www.studylight.org/language-studies/greek-thoughts.html?article=3; https://www.internationalstandardbible.com/M/mystery.html; https://spiritandtruthonline.org/mystery-or-sacred-secret/

30. A Church temple preparation manual says, "In a symbolic way, the teachings and rituals of the temple take us on an upward journey toward eternal life, ending with a symbolic entrance into the presence of God. The characters depicted, the physical setting, the clothing worn, the signs given, and all the events covered in the temple are symbolic" (*Endowed from on High: Temple Preparation Seminar Teacher's Manual* [Salt Lake City: Intellectual Reserve, 2003], 21).

31. https://www.churchofjesuschrist.org/temples/sacred-temple-clothing?lang=eng.

32. "History, 1838–1856, volume C-1 [2 November 1838–31 July 1842]," 1328, The Joseph Smith Papers, https://www.josephsmithpapers.org/paper-summary/history-1838-1856-volume-c-1-2-november-1838-31-july-1842/502.

33. It should be clarified that, as I wrote in *The Holy Invitation*, there are many ways God manifests Himself to His children, or that they enjoy His presence. Sometimes members sincerely wonder if they are supposed to "see" God in the temple. President Henry B. Eyring taught "that we can 'see' the Savior in the temple in the sense that He becomes no longer unknown to us. President Nelson said this: 'We understand Him. We comprehend His work and His glory. And we begin to feel the infinite impact of His matchless life.'

"If you or I should go to the temple insufficiently pure, we would not be able to see, by the power of the Holy Ghost, the spiritual teaching about the Savior that we can receive in the temple." ("I Love to See the Temple," *Liahona*, May 2021; citing Nelson in *Teachings of Russell M. Nelson* [Salt Lake City: Deseret Book, 2018), 36.

NOTES

34. While writing this book, some aspects of the temple endowment clothing were changed for ease of use and cost for members. See letter from the First Presidency, "Adjustments in Temple Ceremonial Clothing," January 17, 2020.
35. You may have heard there is some overlap between aspects of the temple endowment ceremony and freemasonry. Freemasonry is a religious fraternity that developed in Europe in the middle ages as a trade guild wherein brick and stone masons supported and taught one another in their craft and lives. It gradually developed to include religious themes and orders, and by the 1700s was an esoteric fraternity that many men joined (including notable Americans like George Washington and Benjamin Franklin) to build moral character, learn divine truths, and create brotherly connections in the community. Joseph Smith became a freemason in Nauvoo in March 1842. History is clear, however, that many of the major elements of the temple endowment were introduced years before Joseph Smith became a freemason, such as washing and anointing in Kirtland, keys to detecting true and false spirits, covenants such as consecration, Creation themes from the Book of Abraham, the potential to become priests and kings to God, and the power to part the veil to come into God's presence. Notable parallels yet exist between the temple endowment ceremony and aspects found in freemasonry. Although it is not definitive why overlap exists, there are two generally accepted theories. I summarize them as the "apostasy" and "adoption" theories. The apostasy theory is that freemasonry is an apostatized version of ancient temple endowment rituals, and Joseph Smith restored them to their original and higher purpose. The adoption theory is that, after becoming a mason, Joseph Smith adopted and altered effective masonic elements and used them to condense and communicate eternal concepts that had been revealed to him throughout his prophetic ministry. Either theory, or a combination of the two, is possible. Regardless, God authorized the modern ceremony through His key-holding prophet, Joseph Smith, and his subsequent successors. If you would like to learn more, see "Masonry" in Church History Topics (https://www.lds.org/study/history/topics/masonry?lang=eng) or the Church's video "Joseph Smith and Masonry," available on YouTube. See also Steven C. Harper, "Freemasonry and the LDS Temple Endowment," in *A Reason for Faith* (Provo, UT: Religious Studies Center/Deseret Book, 2016).

NOTES

36. While writing this book, some endowment ceremony changes were made, with the First Presidency writing, "Through inspiration, the methods of instruction in the temple experience have changed many times, even in recent history, to help members better understand and live what they learn in the temple. . . . With a concern for all and a desire to enhance the temple learning experience, recent changes have been authorized to the temple endowment ceremony" ("A Message from the First Presidency on Changes to the Temple Endowment," July 20, 2020; https://newsroom.churchofjesuschrist.org/article/first-presidency-temple-message-july-2020).
37. Even standardized ordinances like baptism have changed. Alma's baptismal prayer in the Book of Mormon (see Mosiah 18:13) is notably different than the one Christ later directed the Nephites to use (see 3 Nephi 11:24–25).
38. Brigham Young said that there is a difference between having "knowledge" of the endowment and to "know the *meaning* of the word *endowment*. To know, they must experience" ("Necessity of Building Temples, Etc." *Journal of Discourses*, Apr. 6, 1853, 2:31; https://contentdm.lib.byu.edu/digital/collection/JournalOfDiscourses3/id/9556).
39. John Taylor, "Blessings of the Saints, etc.," January 17, 1858, *Journal of Discourses*, vol. 6, no. 25.

The White Coat Parable

1. While based in modern reality, the people, places, events, and dialogue in this parable are fictitious, meant to convey spiritual concepts. Any resemblance to any actual person (living or deceased) is unintended and coincidental.
2. The Hippocratic oath is referred to as a "covenant." In a modern version it begins: "I swear to fulfill, to the best of my ability and judgment, this covenant" (https://www.medicinenet.com/script/main/art.asp?articlekey=20909).
3. "The White Coat Ceremony was originated by the Arnold P. Gold Foundation specifically for entering medical students. At the ceremony, students are welcomed by their deans, the president of the hospital, or other respected leaders who represent the value system of the school and the new profession the students are about to enter. The white coat is placed on each student's shoulders by individuals who believe in the students' ability to carry on the noble tradition of doctoring" (https://students-residents.aamc.org/choosing-medical

NOTES

-career/article/what-its-participate-white-coat-ceremony/). While many medical schools conduct an official white coat ceremony, there are different ways, words, and orders that things are presented at various white coat ceremonies, depending on the institution's traditions.
4. See https://students-residents.aamc.org/choosing-medical-career/article/what-its-participate-white-coat-ceremony/.
5. Hippocratic Oath taken from New York Medical College, https://www.nymc.edu/commencement/history-awards-and-traditions/som-hippocratic-oath/.
6. Some of the dialogue in this fictionalized ceremony was summarized, paraphrased, or quoted from the White Coat Ceremony of Columbia's Vagelos College of Physicians and Surgeons held Aug. 22, 2019, featuring Dr. Lisa Mellman, Chaplain Janelle Davis, Dr. Lee Goldman, and Dr. Gerald Thomson. Available at https://www.youtube.com/watch?v=HgmUA-k6o6Y.
7. This is an adapted story from a real medical situation, described by Dr. Peter Provonost on "Doctors Confess Their Fatal Mistakes," Joe Kita, *The Healthy*, Aug. 20, 2019; https://www.thehealthy.com/healthcare/doctors/doctors-confess-their-fatal-mistakes/.
8. I'm referencing Elder (and medical doctor) Dale G. Renlund here, who said, "Just as doing 'my-way' medicine leads to morbidity and mortality, doing it 'my way' in life leads to spiritual morbidity and mortality. There is only one true way, and that's God's way" (as cited in "Elder Renlund Speaks to Fellow Physicians on Lessons Learned from His Patients," *Church News*, Oct. 12, 2016, https://www.churchofjesuschrist.org/church/news/elder-renlund-speaks-to-fellow-physicians-on-lessons-learned-from-his-patients?lang=eng).
9. This story and final quote is taken directly from Elder Dale G. Renlund, "Do Justly, Love Mercy, and Walk Humbly with God," *Ensign*, Nov. 2020. The only change is in the name, from "Dr. Jones" to "Dr. James," to fit the character in this story.

The Why of Covenants

1. See Elder Tad R. Callister discuss these powers in more detail in his talk "Our Identity and our Destiny," BYU Education Week Devotional, August 14, 2012, https://speeches.byu.edu/talks/tad-r-callister/our-identity-and-our-destiny/.
2. Elder D. Todd Christofferson said that "our access to [God's] power is through our covenants with Him. . . . In these divine agreements, God binds Himself to sustain, sanctify, and exalt us in return for our

NOTES

commitment to serve Him" ("The Power of Covenants," *Ensign*, May 2009, 20).

3. See President Julie B. Beck, "Teaching the Doctrine of the Family," Address to CES Religious Educators, 2009, 3.
4. President Russell M. Nelson said, "If families were not sealed in holy temples, the whole earth would be utterly wasted" ("The Atonement," *Ensign*, Nov. 1996).
5. Quoted by Rabbi Jonathan Sacks's conversation with David Brooks on "Making Love Last (Va'etchanan 5778)," July 23, 2018, https://rabbisacks.org/making-love-last-vaetchanan-5778-2/.
6. Dale G. Renlund and Ruth L. Renlund, *The Melchizedek Priesthood: Understanding the Doctrine, Living the Principles* (Salt Lake City: Deseret Book, 2018), 56.
7. See Tim Tebow, "If You're Someone Who Always Listens to Their Emotions, You Need to Stop," https://timtebow.com/blog/leading-conviction.
8. C. S. Lewis, *Mere Christianity* (New York: Harper Collins, 2001), 140–41.
9. Dieter F. Uchtdorf, "The Infinite Power of Hope," *Ensign*, Nov. 2008.
10. See James E. Faust, "Where Is the Church?," Devotional address, Brigham Young University, Mar. 1, 2005, 8.
11. "Levi Richards, Journal, 11 June 1843, extract," [16], https://www.josephsmithpapers.org/paper-summary/levi-richards-journal-11-june-1843-extract/2. In 1833 Joseph Smith wrote that the reason for the Restoration was because "the Christian world . . . [had] changed the ordinances and broken the everlasting covenant" ("Letter to Noah C. Saxton, 4 January 1833," 16, The Joseph Smith Papers, https://www.josephsmithpapers.org/paper-summary/letter-to-noah-c-saxton-4-january-1833/3).
12. "In the Church, an ordinance is a sacred, formal act or ceremony performed by the authority of the priesthood" ("Ordinances," Gospel Topics, https://www.churchofjesuschrist.org/study/manual/gospel-topics/ordinances?lang=eng).
13. There are some ordinances, like a baby blessing or a patriarchal blessing, that are not associated with a covenant and are not considered essential ordinances for salvation or exaltation.
14. Robert D. Hales, "Coming to Ourselves: The Sacrament, the Temple, and Sacrifice in Service" (*Ensign*, May 2012).
15. For example, former Relief Society General President Bonnie D.

NOTES

Parkin taught: "So often we talk of making and keeping covenants, but exactly what are they? . . . In the temple, we further covenant to be obedient, to sacrifice, to keep ourselves worthily pure, to contribute to the spreading of truth, to be chaste, to pray, to live the gospel, and to be forever faithful" ("Celebrating Covenants," *Ensign*, May 1995). See also Ezra Taft Benson, "A Vision and a Hope for the Youth of Zion," BYU devotional, April 12, 1977; *The Teachings of Ezra Taft Benson*, 251; "Lesson 4: Receiving Temple Ordinances and Covenants," *Endowed from on High: Temple Preparation Seminar Teacher's Manual*, 16; James E. Talmage, *The House of the Lord*, rev. ed. [1976], 84; Gordon B. Hinckley, *Teachings of Gordon B. Hinckley*, 148; *Preparing to Enter the Holy Temple*, 35.

16. David A. Bednar, "Prepared to Obtain Every Needful Thing," *Ensign*, May 2019.
17. See https://www.churchofjesuschrist.org/temples/prophetic-teachings-on-temples?lang=eng.
18. See *General Handbook* (2021), section 27.2.
19. It can be argued that the obligations to wear the garment and not disclose certain sacred teachings are also covenants, as they are part of the overall covenant commitments embodied in the endowment. Some statements, as referenced in the chapter on the garment, refer to wearing the temple garment as a covenant. However, because the five major laws of the temple endowment are typically grouped as the covenants of the endowment in Church publications, I have patterned my wording to reflect that of the Church's.

Part II: The Covenants

"Discourse, 11 June 1843–A, as Reported by Wilford Woodruff," [43], The Joseph Smith Papers, https://www.josephsmithpapers.org/paper-summary/discourse-11-june-1843-a-as-reported-by-wilford-woodruff/2.

The Commitment to Wear the Garment

1. The *General Handbook* calls the wearing of the garment a covenant: "Members who receive the endowment make a covenant to wear the temple garment throughout their lives" ("Wearing and Caring for the Garment," section 38.5.5). While some places in Church literature call it a covenant, others seem to not use covenantal language, saying one is "obligated to wear it" ("Temples," *True to the Faith*, https://www.churchofjesuschrist.org/study/manual/true-to-the

NOTES

-faith/temples?lang=eng) or calling it a "reminder" of our covenants ("Garments," Gospel Topics, https://www.churchofjesuschrist.org /study/manual/gospel-topics/garments?lang=eng).

2. President Russell M. Nelson taught, "It is understood that each adult temple patron will wear the sacred garment of the priesthood under their regular clothing. This is symbolic of an inner commitment to strive each day to become more like the Lord. It also reminds us to remain faithful each day to covenants made and to walk on the covenant path each day in a higher and holier way" ("Closing Remarks," *Ensign*, Nov. 2019).

3. "Garments," Gospel Topics, https://www.churchofjesuschrist.org /study/manual/gospel-topics/garments?lang=eng; see also Carlos E. Asay, "The Temple Garment: 'An Outward Expression of an Inward Commitment,'" *Ensign*, Aug. 1997.

4. First Presidency Letter, "Preparing to Enter the Temple," Oct. 6, 2019, https://newsroom.churchofjesuschrist.org/multimedia/file /first-presidency-temple-recommend-letter.pdf.

5. This is part of the published temple recommend questions. See https:// newsroom.churchofjesuschrist.org/multimedia/file/first-presidency -temple-recommend-letter.pdf. President Russell M. Nelson read these publicly in his closing remarks at the October 2019 general conference (see "Closing Remarks," *Ensign*, Nov. 2019).

6. These "simple marks" remind of "an orientation toward the gospel principles of obedience, truth, life, and discipleship in Christ" (Evelyn T. Marshall, "Garments," in *Encyclopedia of Mormonism*, ed. Daniel H. Ludlow, 5 vols. [1992], 2:534. Cited in Carlos E. Asay, "The Temple Garment: 'An Outward Expression of an Inward Commitment,'" *Ensign*, Aug. 1997).

7. This analogy was given by President Boyd K. Packer. It is also used in the *Encyclopedia of Mormonism* entry "Garments" (see https://eom .byu.edu/index.php/Garments).

8. Linda S. Reeves, "Worthy of Our Promised Blessings," *Ensign*, Nov. 2015.

9. Boyd K. Packer, *The Holy Temple* (Salt Lake City: Bookcraft, 1980), 75. See also Boyd K. Packer, "The Holy Temple," *Ensign*, Oct. 2010.

10. Russell M. Nelson, "Personal Preparation for Temple Blessings," *Ensign*, May 2001; see also Carlos E. Asay, "The Temple Garment: 'An Outward Expression of an Inward Commitment,'" *Ensign*, Aug. 1997.

NOTES

11. "When you wear [the temple garment] properly, it provides protection against temptation and evil" ("Temples," *True to the Faith* [2004]).
12. "The promise of protection and blessings is conditioned upon worthiness and faithfulness in keeping the covenant" (First Presidency Letter, 10 Oct. 1988). Similar language is used by the First Presidency and Church today: "Remember that the blessings that are related to this sacred privilege [of wearing the temple garment] depend on your worthiness and your faithfulness in keeping temple covenants" ("Temples," *True to the Faith*). The *General Handbook* uses the same language (see "Temple Clothing and Garments," section 38.8.49).
13. "In our day the garment encourages modesty, but its significance is much deeper" (Gospel Topics Essay, "Garments," https://www.church ofjesuschrist.org/study/manual/gospel-topics/garments?lang=eng).
14. First Presidency Letter, 10 Oct. 1988.
15. Brigham Young, "Southern Missions, Etc." *Journal of Discourses*, 12:297.
16. See Russell M. Nelson, "The Sabbath is a Delight," *Ensign*, May 2015.
17. Elder David A. Bednar taught, "In the ordinances of the holy temple we more completely and fully take upon us the name of Jesus Christ" ("Honorably Hold a Name and Standing," *Ensign*, May 2009.
18. Russell M. Nelson, "The Atonement," *Ensign*, Nov. 1996.

The Promise to Not Reveal Sacred Teachings

1. "Journal, December 1841–December 1842," 94, The Joseph Smith Papers, https://www.josephsmithpapers.org/paper-summary/journal-december-1841-december-1842/25.
2. Heber C. Kimball to Parley P. Pratt, 17 June 1842, Church History Library. Cited in "Temple Endowment," Gospel Topics, source #4, https://www.churchofjesuschrist.org/study/history/topics/temple-endowment?lang=eng.
3. James E. Talmage wrote of the endowment in 1912, "This course of instruction includes a recital of the most prominent events of the creative period, the condition of our first parents in the Garden of Eden, their disobedience and consequent expulsion from that blissful abode, their condition in the lone and dreary world when doomed to live by labor and sweat" (The House of the Lord: A Study of Holy Sanctuaries Ancient and Modern [Salt Lake City: The Deseret News, 1912], 99–100; see also "Endowed with Covenants and Blessings," *Ensign*, Feb. 1995).

NOTES

4. "Commonly Asked Questions," *Ensign*, Oct. 2010.
5. "Understanding Our Covenants with God," *Ensign,* July 2012.
6. "Commonly Asked Questions," *Ensign*, Oct. 2010.
7. "Temple Endowment Q&A," *Liahona*, Mar. 2019.
8. David A. Bednar, "Prepared to Obtain Every Needful Thing," *Ensign*, May 2019.
9. "Temple Endowment," Gospel Topics, https://www.churchofjesus christ.org/study/history/topics/temple-endowment?lang=eng.
10. "About the Temple Endowment." https://www.churchofjesuschrist .org/temples/what-is-temple-endowment?lang=eng; see also James E. Talmage, *House of the Lord: A Study of Holy Sanctuaries Ancient and Modern* (Salt Lake City: The Church of Jesus Christ of Latter-day Saints, 1912), 99–100.
11. "History, 1838–1856, volume C-1 Addenda," 46, The Joseph Smith Papers, https://www.josephsmithpapers.org/paper-summary/history -1838-1856-volume-c-1-addenda/46.

The Law of Obedience

1. "Obedience is the first law of heaven" (*Preach My Gospel*, "Chapter 6: How Do I Develop Christlike Attributes?" [Salt Lake City: Intellectual Reserve, 2004], 122).
2. Elder Jeffrey R. Holland taught Saints in Manila, "Obedience is . . . the first covenant that we make in the temple" (*Newsroom*, "Elder Jeffrey R. Holland Visits Philippines, Shares Message on Love," Jan. 14, 2019, https://news-ph.churchofjesuschrist.org/article/elder -jeffrey-r--holland-visits-philippines--shares-message-on-love).
3. See Bruce R. McConkie, *Mormon Doctrine* (Salt Lake City: Bookcraft, 1958), 539.
4. Brigham Young, "The Earth the Home of Man, Etc.," *Journal of Discourses* 10:299.
5. "The word *law* in a gospel sense refers to the statutes, judgments, and principles of salvation revealed by the Lord to man" ("Section 42, The Law of the Lord," *Doctrine and Covenants Student Manual* [2002], 82). For an interesting verse on prophets *creating* laws on earth and in heaven, read carefully Doctrine and Covenants 128:9.
6. See https://www.etymonline.com/word/obedience#etymonline_v _30944.
7. See https://www.etymonline.com/word/faithful#etymonline_v _32950.
8. See https://www.etymonline.com/word/keep#etymonline_v_1798.

NOTES

9. The degree to which laws of God remain fixed and immutable, like scientific laws of gravity, is a debated point. See President Boyd K. Packer, "The Great Plan of Happiness," address to religious educators, Brigham Young University, Aug. 10, 1993, https://www.churchofjesuschrist.org/study/manual/teaching-seminary-preservice-readings-religion-370-471-and-475/the-great-plan-of-happiness?lang=eng.
10. See Erastus Snow, "Mental Improvement and Spiritual Advancement, Etc." *Journal of Discourses*, 8:215.
11. See Orson Pratt, "Interest Manifested, Etc." *Journal of Discourses*, 17:103.
12. Today, not only is adherence to the Word of Wisdom required to enter a temple, but persons cannot be baptized unless they "live the word of wisdom" (*Preach My Gospel*, 2004, 204).
13. See Orson Pratt, *Journal of Discourses*, 16:158–59.
14. See "Plural Marriage in The Church of Jesus Christ of Latter-day Saints," Gospel Topics, https://www.churchofjesuschrist.org/study/manual/gospel-topics/plural-marriage-in-the-church-of-jesus-christ-of-latter-day-saints?lang=eng; see also the *General Handbook* 32.6.2.5, which states that a "membership council is required" for "plural marriage."
15. "This living document [D&C 42] continues to serve as a law of the Church Jesus Christ" ("The Law," *Revelations in Context*, https://www.churchofjesuschrist.org/study/manual/revelations-in-context/the-law?lang=eng).
16. The *General Handbook* says that "in matters of doctrine and Church policy, the authoritative sources are the scriptures, the teachings of the living prophets, and the *General Handbook*" (Section 38.8.45).
17. See L. Tom Perry, "When Ye Are Prepared, Ye Shall Not Fear," Ensign, Nov. 1981.
18. See David A. Bednar, "The Windows of Heaven," *Ensign*, Nov. 2013; see also Gordon B. Hinckley, "This Thing Was Not Done in a Corner," *Ensign*, Nov. 1996.
19. See L. Tom Perry, "Nauvoo—A Demonstration of Faith," *Ensign*, May 1980.
20. See James E. Faust, "Search Me, O God, and Know My Heart," *Ensign*, May 1998.
21. "Letter to Martin Harris, 22 February 1831," [1], The Joseph Smith Papers, https://www.josephsmithpapers.org/paper-summary/letter-to-martin-harris-22-february-1831/1.

NOTES

22. "Letter to the Church, circa February 1834," 136, https://www.josephsmithpapers.org/paper-summary/letter-to-the-church-circa-february-1834/2; see also D&C 93:1.

The Law of Sacrifice

1. President Russell M. Nelson taught, "Thus, the laws of obedience and sacrifice are indelibly intertwined" ("Lessons from Eve," *Ensign*, Nov. 1987).
2. "The law of sacrifice provides an opportunity for us to prove to the Lord that we love Him more than any other thing" (M. Russell Ballard, "The Law of Sacrifice," *Ensign*, Oct. 1998).
3. The *General Handbook* defines part of "the law of sacrifice" as "repenting with a broken heart and contrite spirit" (27.2).
4. See Russell M. Nelson, "Let God Prevail," *Ensign*, Nov. 2020.
5. See Neal A. Maxwell, "Swallowed Up in the Will of the Father," *Ensign*, Nov. 1995.
6. See Neal A. Maxwell, "Deny Yourselves of All Ungodliness," *Ensign*, May 1995.
7. See M. Russell Ballard, "The Law of Sacrifice," *Ensign*, Oct. 1998. See also Dieter F. Uchtdorf, "Come, Join with Us," *Ensign*, Nov. 2013.
8. "Doctrine and Covenants, 1835," 60, The Joseph Smith Papers, https://www.josephsmithpapers.org/paper-summary/doctrine-and-covenants-1835/68.
9. Religion sociologist Rodney Stark, who describes the Church as being a "demanding faith," concluded that higher-demanding faiths produce higher commitment (see Rodney Stark, *The Rise of Mormonism* [New York: Columbia University Press, 2005], 94).
10. "An acceptable sacrifice is when we give up something good for something of far greater worth" (Dieter F. Uchtdorf, "Forget Me Not," *Ensign*, Nov. 2011).
11. See Gordon B. Hinckley, "Life's Obligations," *Ensign*, Feb. 1999; see also "Excerpts from Recent Addresses of President Gordon B. Hinckley," *Ensign*, Sept. 1997.

The Law of the Gospel

1. The *General Handbook* defines the "law of the gospel" as following "the higher law that He taught while He was on the earth" (27.2). "This higher law is meant to be lived because we trust the Savior and want to become like Him" (Eleanor Cain Adams and Allisa White,

NOTES

"Living the Law of Chastity in a Dating World Full of Gray Areas," *Ensign*, Aug. 2020).

2. Bible Dictionary, "Gospels, " https://www.churchofjesuschrist.org/study/scriptures/bd/gospels?lang=eng.
3. See Gordon B. Hinckley, "The Favored Season," *Ensign*, Sept. 1995.
4. "A more comprehensive and accurate listing is found in 3 Ne. 12:1–12" (Bible Dictionary, "Beatitudes," https://www.churchofjesuschrist.org/study/scriptures/bd/beatitudes?lang=eng).
5. For a comprehensive and well-written article on appropriate humor, see Peter B. Rawlins, "A Serious Look at Humor," *New Era*, Aug. 1974.
6. Joseph Smith called himself "playful and cheerful" ("History, 1838–1856, volume D-1 [1 August 1842–1 July 1843]," 1563, The Joseph Smith Papers, https://www.josephsmithpapers.org/paper-summary/history-1838-1856-volume-d-1-1-august-1842-1-july-1843/206).
7. "History, 1838–1856, volume C-1 [2 November 1838–31 July 1842] [b]," 904[b], The Joseph Smith Papers, https://www.josephsmithpapers.org/paper-summary/history-1838-1856-volume-c-1-2-november-1838-31-july-1842/86.
8. Elder Richard G. Scott taught, "Another principle is to be cautious with humor. Loud, inappropriate laughter will offend the Spirit. A good sense of humor helps revelation; loud laughter does not. A sense of humor is an escape valve for the pressures of life. Another enemy to revelation comes from exaggeration or loudness in what is stated. Careful, quiet speech will favor the receipt of revelation" ("How to Obtain Revelation and Inspiration for Your Personal Life," *Ensign*, May 2012).
9. *Preparing to Enter the Holy Temple* says we should talk in the temple in "a very quiet and subdued tone. Loud talking and loud laughter are not fitting in the house of the Lord" (7).
10. "Journal, 1835–1836[a]," 151[a], The Joseph Smith Papers, https://www.josephsmithpapers.org/paper-summary/journal-1835-1836/152.
11. President Russell M. Nelson asked BYU students, "If you have made sacred covenants in the temple, how do you react when you hear evil-speaking of the Lord's anointed?" ("Integrity of the Heart," BYU Speeches, February 23, 1993, https://speeches.byu.edu/talks/russell-m-nelson/integrity-heart/).
12. See Dallin H. Oaks, "Criticism," *Ensign*, Feb. 1987.

NOTES

13. The Bible Dictionary describes the Beatitudes as "certain elements that go to form the refined and spiritual character, all of which will be present whenever that character exists in its perfection. Rather than being isolated statements, the Beatitudes are interrelated and progressive in their arrangement" (Bible Dictionary, "Beatitudes," https://www.churchofjesuschrist.org/study/scriptures/bd/beatitudes?lang=eng).
14. "In his Sermon on the Mount the Master has given us somewhat of a revelation of his own character . . . and in so doing has given us a blueprint for our own lives" (Harold B. Lee, *Decisions for Successful Living* [Salt Lake City: Deseret Book, 1973], 55–56).

The Law of Chastity

1. See *General Handbook* (2020), 2.1.2; see also David A. Bednar, "We Believe in Being Chaste," *Ensign*, May 2013, or Dale G. Renlund and Ruth L. Renlund, "The Divine Purposes of Sexual Intimacy," *Ensign*, Aug. 2020.
2. *General Handbook*, 21.2.
3. "The Family: A Proclamation to the World," *Ensign*, Nov. 2010.
4. See *General Handbook*, 2.1.2, and *For the Strength of Youth*, "Sexual Purity."
5. M. Russell Ballard, "Fathers and Sons: A Remarkable Relationship," *Ensign*, Nov. 2009.
6. David A. Bednar, "We Believe in Being Chaste," *Ensign*, May 2013.
7. See then–BYU President Jeffrey R. Holland, "Of Souls, Symbols, and Sacraments," BYU Speeches, January 12, 1988, https://speeches.byu.edu/talks/jeffrey-r-holland/souls-symbols-sacraments/.
8. The *General Handbook* says, "Tenderness and respect—not selfishness—should guide [a husband and wife's] intimate relationship" (2.1.2).
9. Sister Ruth L. Renlund and her husband, Elder Dale G. Renlund, have said, "The law of chastity is an eternal law, given by our Heavenly Father to all His children in all ages." They use words like "trust," "devotion," "consideration," and "respect," saying that intimacy should not be used "to control or dominate" ("The Divine Purposes of Sexual Intimacy," *Ensign*, Aug. 2020).
10. See Chelom E. Leavitt, "Conversations about Intimacy and Sex That Can Prepare You for Marriage," *Ensign*, Aug. 2020 (digital only).
11. Adam Miller, *Letters to a Young Mormon* (Provo, UT: Neal A. Maxwell Institute for Religious Scholarship, 2014), 64.

NOTES

12. Dallin H. Oaks said, "The power to create mortal life is the most exalted power God has given his children" ("The Great Plan of Happiness," *Ensign,* Nov. 1993).

The Law of Consecration

1. Portions of this chapter are adapted from "Inviting the Presence of God" from my book *Seekers Wanted* (Salt Lake City: Deseret Book, 2019), 140–44.
2. President Gordon B. Hinckley said, "The law of sacrifice and the law of consecration have not been done away with and are still in effect" (*Teachings of Gordon B. Hinckley*, 639).
3. "The law of consecration," said scholar Hugh Nibley, is "the consummation of the laws of obedience and sacrifice" and "the threshold of the celestial kingdom" ("Approaching Zion," vol. 9 of *The Collected Works of Hugh Nibley* [1989], 168; see also *Teachings of Ezra Taft Benson*, 121).
4. Elder D. Todd Christofferson said that "true success in this life comes in consecrating our lives—that is, our time and choices—to God's purposes" ("Reflections on a Consecrated Life,*" Ensign*, Nov. 2010.
5. For a good historical review of the different ways the law of consecration has been implemented in the past, see Casey P. Griffiths, "'A Covenant and a Deed Which Cannot Be Broken': The Continuing Saga of Consecration," in *Foundations of the Restoration: Fulfillment of the Covenant Purposes* (Provo, UT: BYU Religious Studies Center, 2016), https://rsc.byu.edu/foundations-restoration/covenant-deed-which-cannot-be-broken.
6. The *General Handbook* explains that "in the endowment, members are invited to make sacred covenants to . . . keep the law of consecration, which means dedicating their time, talents, and everything with which the Lord has blessed them to building up Jesus Christ's Church on the earth" (27.2). See also *Teachings of Ezra Taft Benson*, 121; Bruce R. McConkie, "Obedience, Consecration, and Sacrifice," *Ensign*, May 1975.
7. See Merriam-Webster, "Consecrate," https://www.merriam-webster.com/dictionary/consecrate.
8. *Preparing to Enter the Holy Temple,* 35; see also *Teachings of Ezra Taft Benson,* 121.
9. See D. Todd Christofferson, "Reflections on a Consecrated Life," where he mentioned five aspects of living a consecrated life, including

NOTES

"purity, work, respect for one's physical body, service, and integrity" (*Ensign*, Nov. 2010).

10. For an extended explanation on this idea, see "Seeking Zion" in my book *Seekers Wanted* (Salt Lake City: Deseret Book, 2019), 147–52.
11. "Until one abides by the laws of obedience, sacrifice, the gospel, and chastity, he cannot abide the law of consecration, which is the law pertaining to the celestial kingdom" (*Teachings of Ezra Taft Benson*, 121).
12. The original 1831 revelation says, "Behold thou shalt conscrate all thy property properties that which thou hast unto me with a covena[n]t and Deed which cannot be broken" ("Revelation, 9 February 1831 [D&C 42:1–72]," [3], The Joseph Smith Papers, https://www.josephsmithpapers.org/paper-summary/revelation-9-february-1831-dc-421-72/3). By the 1835 edition of the Doctrine and Covenants, it was changed from "all thy properties" to "of thy properties" (see "Doctrine and Covenants, 1835," 122, The Joseph Smith Papers, https://www.josephsmithpapers.org/paper-summary/doctrine-and-covenants-1835/130).
13. Steven Harper describes these as "Agency, Stewardship, and Accountability." Mine are a derivative of his, but I am indebted to his original breakdown and am building off his earlier writings. See "All Things are the Lord's: The Law of Consecration in the Doctrine and Covenants," *The Doctrine and Covenants: Revelations in Context*, ed. Andrew H. Hedges, J. Spencer Fluhman, and Alonzo L. Gaskill (Provo and Salt Lake City: Religious Studies Center, Brigham Young University and Deseret Book, 2008), 212–28.
14. See http://www.thefreedictionary.com/agency.
15. Elder David A. Bednar taught, "Morning and evening prayers—and all of the prayers in between—are not unrelated, discrete events; rather, they are linked together," including reporting to God in our evening prayers "the events of the day" and rededicating the next day to do His will ("Pray Always," *Ensign*, Nov. 2008).
16. An article in *For the Strength of Youth* defines consecration as "a principle the Lord gives to His covenant people" to dedicate "their time, talents, and material resources to serve the Lord, His Church, and His children" ("What is the law of consecration? How does it affect me?" Apr. 2021).

NOTES

Part III: The Power

"History, 1838–1856, volume E-1 [1 July 1843–30 April 1844]," 1708, The Joseph Smith Papers, 2020, https://www.josephsmithpapers.org/paper-summary/history-1838-1856-volume-e-1-1-july-1843-30-april-1844/80.

The Endowment of Power

1. Remember, as part of the first endowment of power at the June 1831 conference, Joseph Smith had learned while translating the Bible that high priests had power to "break mountains" and "divide the seas" and "put at defiance the armies of nations" (JST, Genesis 14:30–31). Editors for *The Joseph Smith Papers* write, "Jared Carter, for instance, associated the ability to perform miraculous healings with those ordained to the high priesthood" at the endowment of power at the June 1831 conference (Carter, Journal, 16–17). ("Historical Introduction for the Minutes, circa 3–4 June 1831," 4, The Joseph Smith Papers, https://www.josephsmithpapers.org/paper-summary/minutes-circa-3-4-june-1831/2).

2. At the June 1831 conference at the first endowment of high priestly power, there were both heavenly manifestations and evil ones. "The Devil took occation, to make known his power," said John Whitmer in his history of the event, and Joseph Smith "commanded the devil in the name of Christ and he departed" ("John Whitmer, History, 1831–circa 1847," 29, The Joseph Smith Papers, https://www.josephsmithpapers.org/paper-summary/john-whitmer-history-1831-circa-1847/33). At the conclusion of the June 1831 conference, the Lord gave a revelation, giving "a pattern in all things, that ye may not be deceived" (D&C 52:14). In verses 15–19 He expounded on that pattern, related to obeying certain ordinances. This pivotal event, and others (such as keys that Adam gave "detecting the devil when he appear[s] as an angel of light" [D&C 128:20; see also D&C 129]), are subsumed into greater temple concepts related to discerning truth from error.

3. The *General Handbook* summarizes "some of the gifts that members receive through the temple endowment" as "greater knowledge of the Lord's purposes and teachings" and "increased hope, comfort, and peace" (27.2).

4. See Dieter F. Uchtdorf, "Your Potential, Your Privilege," *Ensign*, May

2014; Joseph B. Wirthlin, "The Unspeakable Gift," *Ensign*, May 2003.
5. See James E. Faust, "Lost Horizons," *Ensign*, Aug. 1999.
6. Relief Society General President Jean B. Bingham, in a discussion with Church President Russell M. Nelson on the oath and covenant of the priesthood found in Doctrine and Covenants 84, commented, "So that is just as relevant to women as it is to men, because all those priesthood blessings from the oath and covenant of the priesthood are enjoyed by both men and women." To which President Nelson responded, "Totally. . . . Exactly, exactly" (author's transcript taken from https://www.churchofjesuschrist.org/media/video/2020-05-0280-the-oath-and-covenant-of-the-priesthood-is-relevant-to-women?lang=eng).
7. President Russell M. Nelson has taught, "No man in this Church can obtain the highest degree of celestial glory without a worthy woman who is sealed to him. This temple ordinance enables eventual exaltation for both of them" ("Salvation and Exaltation," *Ensign*, May 2008).
8. See *General Handbook* (2.1). President Dallin H. Oaks taught, "The Lord has promised that in the eternities no blessing will be denied his sons and daughters who keep the commandments, are true to their covenants, and desire what is right" ("The Great Plan of Happiness," *Ensign*, Nov. 1993).
9. BYU Religion professor Richard Bennett writes, "The endowment was in many ways a precursor to the eternal union of man and woman—celestial marriage" (*Temples Rising* [Provo, UT: BYU Religious Studies Center/Deseret Book, 2019], 83).
10. See *General Handbook* 2.1.1.

The Taste of Eternity

1. "I Am used here in the Greek is identical with the Septuagint usage in Ex. 3:14 which identifies Jehovah" (John 8:58, footnote b).
2. The name *Moses*, of Hebrew origin, means "to draw out," likely "because I drew him out of the water," as the daughter of Pharaoh is ascribed to have said (Exodus 2:10; see footnote 10b).
3. "The initiatory ordinances include special blessings regarding your divine heritage and potential. As part of these ordinances, you will also be authorized to wear the sacred temple garment" ("About the Temple Endowment," https://www.churchofjesuschrist.org/temples/what-is-temple-endowment?lang=eng).

NOTES

4. Ezra Taft Benson taught, "In the course of our visits to the temple, we are given insights into the meaning of the eternal journey of man. We see beautiful and impressive symbolisms of the most important events—past, present, and future—symbolizing man's mission in relationship to God. We are reminded of our obligations as we make solemn covenants pertaining to obedience, consecration, sacrifice, and dedicated service to our Heavenly Father" (*The Teachings of Ezra Taft Benson*, 251).
5. "Discourse, 7 April 1844, as Reported by Times and Seasons," 613, The Joseph Smith Papers, https://www.josephsmithpapers.org/paper-summary/discourse-7-april-1844-as-reported-by-times-and-seasons/2.
6. *Teachings of Russell M. Nelson*, 373.
7. President Russell M. Nelson taught, "We feel part of something greater than ourselves. Our inborn yearnings for family connections are fulfilled when we are linked to our ancestors through sacred ordinances of the temple" ("Generations Linked in Love," *Ensign*, May 2010).
8. See Quentin L. Cook, "Roots and Branches," *Ensign*, May 2014.
9. John Taylor, "Men Eternal Beings, Etc.," *Journal of Discourses* (Conference Report, April 1854), vol. 1, no. 53.

ABOUT THE AUTHOR

ANTHONY SWEAT is an associate professor of Church history and doctrine at Brigham Young University. He is the author of numerous best-selling books related to the history and teachings of The Church of Jesus Christ of Latter-day Saints and a regular speaker at Latter-day Saint events and conferences. He received a BFA in painting and drawing from the University of Utah and MEd and PhD degrees in education from Utah State University. He and his wife, Cindy, are parents of seven children and reside in Utah.